The
Weekend
Cookbook

MICHAEL JOSEPH

Published by the Penguin Group

Penguin Books Ltd, 80 Strand, London WC2R 0RL, England

Penguin Group (USA) Inc., 375 Hudson Street, New York, New York 10014, USA

Penguin Group (Canada), 90 Eglinton Avenue East, Suite 700, Toronto, Ontario, Canada M4P 2Y3
(a division of Pearson Penguin Canada Inc.)

Penguin Ireland, 25 St Stephen's Green, Dublin 2, Ireland (a division of Penguin Books Ltd)

Penguin Group (Australia), 250 Camberwell Road,
Camberwell, Victoria 3124, Australia (a division of Pearson Australia Group Pty Ltd)

Penguin Books India Pvt Ltd, 11 Community Centre,
Panchsheel Park, New Delhi – 110 017, India

Penguin Group (NZ), 67 Apollo Drive, Rosedale, Auckland 0632, New Zealand
(a division of Pearson New Zealand Ltd)

Penguin Books (South Africa) (Pty) Ltd, Block D,
Rosebank Office Park, 181 Jan Smuts Avenue, Parktown North, Gauteng 2193, South Africa

Penguin Books Ltd, Registered Offices: 80 Strand, London WC2R 0RL, England

www.penguin.com

First published 2012

1

Copyright © Catherine Hill, 2012

www.theweekendcook.co.uk

The moral right of the author has been asserted

Photographs copyright © Tim Winter

Design by Nathan Burton

Printed in China

A CIP catalogue record for this book is available from the British Library

ISBN: 978-0-718-15909-2

www.greenpenguin.co.uk

MIX
Paper from
responsible sources
FSC™ C018179
www.fsc.org

Penguin Books is committed to a sustainable
future for our business, our readers and our planet.
This book is made from Forest Stewardship
Council™ certified paper.

ALWAYS LEARNING   PEARSON

The Weekend Cookbook

Catherine Hill

Photography by Tim Winter

MICHAEL JOSEPH
an imprint of
Penguin Books

For my wonderful husband and two beautiful children.
This is all for you . . .

Contents

Introduction

Whilst this book was originally written with a weekend away in mind, it is equally valuable as a cookbook for recipes to be enjoyed at home when friends and family come to stay. I hope that it will become an invaluable book for those times when you fancy a weekend of cooking with loved ones and need some inspirational ideas for hassle-free eating.

I reckon the world is pretty much divided into two kinds of people: those who have a weekend away and rarely venture into the kitchen other than to make a brew or a bit of toast and maybe hunt out the bottle opener. And then there are those who love to cook . . .

I undeniably fall into the latter category and, I'm happy to say, so do most of my friends and family. I'm not for one minute suggesting I'm a slave to the kitchen, but I really couldn't imagine a weekend away without great food making an appearance at every opportunity.

As for most people, my perfect weekend away would probably include fish and chips on the beach (and I'm prepared to do this whatever the weather) or a stonking lunch in a snuggly bar with a pint of local beer. But when the opportunity arises, I will always head to the kitchen and cook something glorious for everyone to share.

My approach to food, whether cooked at home or on holiday, is the same as it's always been: simple, relaxed, delicious and without any pretence. In other words, I'm a family cook. I truly believe that the food should suit the mood and do its best to enhance a weekend and it should in no way stop you from having lots of fun.

The trick to getting the balance right for a great weekend away lies in planning ahead (more about that later), sharing the workload and choosing the right food for that particular occasion. There's no point in really going to town on a Friday evening, your first night away in a strange house and an even stranger kitchen. Friday night is all about taking it easy, warming something through that you've made ahead and brought with you. Or why not throw something together from scratch that requires minimal ingredients or do something that might involve a little help from eager friends?

In contrast, Saturday night is the time for getting a bit clever in the kitchen. You'll hopefully have had time to relax and take stock, so doing something that bit posher or trickier might just tickle your fancy.

Whilst all of the chapters are arranged chronologically, from Friday through to Sunday, feel free to dip in and out as the mood takes you. All of the recipes – unless otherwise stated – serve four. I could have written them to serve six but I always think it's easier to do half again for six people, double them up for eight or halve them if you're lucky enough to have a romantic getaway!

Children will love some of these dishes but you know what your kids will and won't go for. No matter what, I always end up packing Weetabix, endless amounts of cheese for toasties, fresh pasta for instant suppers plus a few emergency fish fingers, if only to ensure a bit of peace and normality during the weekend.

Making life easy

Can I just say at this point that you're dealing with a woman who learned the art of efficient food packing and planning the hard way? I spent the first few weeks of a six-month bike tour of New Zealand carrying endless bottles of soy, spices and sauces, packs of noodles, cans of coconut milk and various dried sausages, not to mention the large bottle of fake tan I managed to hide in my husband's pack for several weeks! Needless to say, I very quickly worked out how to carry just the essentials and nothing more. Below is a list of ingredients, tools and tricks that I've discovered through trial and error (via a lot of self-catering trips!) that will hopefully help to make your weekend away that little bit easier.

Make these foods your holiday friends . . .

Ready-made gnocchi
It's a real rib-sticker that tastes just great with big gutsy sauces and ragùs. Just remember to pile on the flavour and season well as it soaks it up like a sponge. Most varieties cook in minutes and one 500g pack will easily serve four hungry adults.

Great-quality pasta
If you're going to choose dried, it's worth investing in a quality brand. I honestly don't think you can beat DeCecco. It costs a little bit more than most pastas, but if you're going to the effort of cooking a really great sauce, why would you pour it over second-rate, flabby pasta? Try it and see what you think.

Ready-made pasta sauces
There are loads out there and it's simply just a question of tasting your way around them and finding your favourites. Once you've made your choice, you can promote them from the simple task of coating pasta and use them elsewhere . . . As toppings for pizza; with a dash of white wine as the base for a cheat's fish stew; or add a splodge to pep up home-made chilli (especially good if you've been heavy-handed with the spices!).

Olives
Good for soaking up one glass of wine too many, but also great finely chopped and turned into a coarse, garlicky home-made tapenade. I use it under the skin of whole roast chickens, stirred into salad dressings for extra oomph or just spread thickly on hot toast.

Oven chips
OK, not the most glamorous of ingredients, but there are some pretty good ones out there now. You know the kids will love them, they're great for padding out a main-course salad if everyone suddenly comes over all ravenous, plus they make the perfect edible ice pack for transporting your food. What's not to love?

Halloumi

I love this stuff and it travels really well. It's great on a barbie, wonderful with salads, yummy with couscous and it makes a pretty good fake paneer cheese should you suddenly feel the need to make a veggie curry.

Chorizo

The whole dried sausages are just perfect if you're travelling long distances as they don't need a jot of refrigeration. They're completely addictive sliced and dry-fried until crisp. Try them in stews, scattered over salads or serve as a near-instant savoury snack.

Lemons and limes

These highly transportable fruit add instant flavour to fish dishes, pasta, salads and anything full of spices. And can you imagine a G&T or Mojito without them?

Herbs

Go for pots of herbs if you need a bit of longevity. Otherwise buy fresh and give them a good dunk in cold water before placing in food bags. When you seal the bags, make sure you keep a little air in them to cushion them for the journey.

Spices

When I know what I'm going to cook, I dispense just enough into little stack-able make-up pots to save transporting the entire kitchen across the country.

Seasoning

It sounds obvious, but I have been to a few holiday cottages that had either no salt and pepper whatsoever or just dusty old white pepper in a shaker and a smidgen of slightly damp salt. Worth packing just in case.

Gravy granules

Gravy does sometimes need that extra little oomph or thickness and who's to know you sprinkled in a few granules at the last minute?

Mascarpone cheese

Instant velvety richness for pasta sauces, soups and dips, or use as a base for creamy home-made fruit fools and desserts.

Oil

I'm quite guilty of using olive oil for everything, but it really is a waste of both flavour and money. Plump for a really lovely extra virgin olive oil when you need that wonderful fruity flavour, but for general cooking and frying go for a simple sunflower oil.

Soy sauce

Kikkoman has the most wonderful, complex flavour that beats other soy sauces hands down. If you want a lighter flavour, combine with a splash of water and a pinch of sugar rather than ferrying two bottles of light and dark around with you.

Ready-made custard

The only thing for pouring over hot puddings but also great for mustering up quick assembly-job trifles, or make a bodge-it ice-cream by mixing with whipped cream and plenty of smushed summer berries before freezing.

Tools and tricks

Scales

Never in a million years would I take a set of scales on holiday with me, and if I did, it would be in the certain knowledge that my husband would throw me out at the first service station! But then there really is no need for scales when you're not going to be making tricky cakes, biscuits or meringues. Instead, use the pack size as a guide when you're cooking, and taste as you go along. As you probably won't have any real spoon measures to hand (i.e. 1 teaspoon = 5ml, 1 tablespoon = 15ml), it's fine to use the spoons from the drawer. None of the recipes are particularly tricky and none of them will be ruined by a little too much of this or too little of that. Just use your best judgement and keep on tasting! Where I have given recipes for a steamed pudding, I've measured it in ml or fluid volume rather than by the gram. I've also included a nifty Yorkshire pudding recipe that uses a standard individual-serving yogurt pot as a measuring device.

Sharp knives

I have to confess I do always take my favourite knife with me as I can't bear the thought of struggling with blunt old knives. They're dangerous as they slip so easily and using a dodgy knife can easily add ten minutes on to your preparation time.

Foil and baking parchment

Folded flat into large squares, they take up no room and weigh nothing. Invaluable for bakes, roasts and barbies.

Food bags

I couldn't imagine a world without them, but they have to be sturdy and they have to be big. They're great for decanting sauces, stews and salads into and they're wonderful for transporting food from home. Just remember to double-bag if you're dealing with anything particularly saucy.

Cool bags

I tend to go for the soft material ones for shorter trips and the sturdy big boxes for anything longer. A base of thick newspaper can help trap the cold and try to them pack as tightly as possible because any air pockets will sap away the cold.

Staying cool

I tend to transport a fair bit of frozen food, which acts as an edible ice pack. Frozen chips, peas, ice cubes, stews and soups all help keep the temperature down. Take care, though, when you pack soft leaves, fruits, herbs or any delicate veggies – if soft-leaved herbs and salads come into direct contact with anything icy (the back of a fridge, an ice pack or a bag of frozen peas), they'll wilt and very quickly turn to a dark mush.

Planning and the art of delegation

If you're holidaying with friends, put your heads together well in advance so that you can plan what each of you is going to cook each day. Not only does it help spread the cost and save on doubling up; it also means that all of you can have a little down time. There's nothing worse than feeling like you're a travelling chef! Once your meals are planned, the shopping and packing list will come naturally. We have a bunch of friends with whom we regularly go away, so we tend to do a joint online shop. We usually start the list a week or so before we go away. That way, we can add what we need, pack what we can and then split the bill fifty–fifty. Everybody's happy!

When it comes to choosing what to cook, go for something that won't leave you in a cold sweat because you've taken on too much. Choose something you feel comfortable with, but most of all make sure you're really going to enjoy cooking and eating it.

If you do fancy more than one course, either split the cooking so each of you makes a separate course or opt for a trickier main course followed by a pudding that requires little more than a quick assembly job from bits you've bought (cream, ready-made meringues and summer fruit for an Eton mess, for instance), or wheel out something you managed to whip up earlier and stash in the fridge (double cream, melted chocolate and Bourbon for the perfect boozy pud!).

Friday night easy

I really love that feeling of arriving at a holiday cottage for the weekend, running around looking into every room, opening cupboards and drawers and getting a fire going if it's a bit cold outside.

It has to be said that the first thing any of my lot do is crack open a bottle of beer or wine to celebrate the start of a weekend away. This is usually followed by the frantic opening of various packets of crisps and snacks, given the drive we've all just endured.

I'd love to say I'm the sort of person who then heads upstairs and starts putting clothes in drawers and on hangers and toiletries in the bathroom, but I'm not. I head to the kitchen and start unpacking all those carefully chosen bits I've squirrelled away to kick off a weekend of great food with friends and family.

That said, Friday night food is all about ease. Whether it's a curry that I've made a day or two before, ready for the stove, or a quick assembly job that results in something quick and delicious, this is not the time for tricky cooking.

If speed and ease is key, I'm not ashamed of using ready-made sauces and I think everyone should have the confidence to cook recipes that require as little as three key ingredients – where's the harm as long as those ingredients are well married and top quality?

For anything that does require a little more time and effort, grab a willing helper and get everyone settled and involved in the kitchen – it's what the best evenings are made of . . .

Easy recipes for a Friday night in

Sausage and porcini *ragù* with gnocchi 21

Sausages cooked with garlic and rosemary. Add a ready-made pasta sauce, rehydrated porcini mushrooms and black olives and serve over hot gnocchi. A great dish to make and take, either frozen or fresh.

Hot-smoked salmon fishcakes with dill and lemon sauce 22

Hot-smoked salmon flaked and mixed with mash, spring onions and parsley. Served with a soured-cream sauce flavoured with lemon and dill. Easy enough to make on the night or make, freeze and take.

Dolcelatte and leek risotto 25

Softened leeks simmered with Arborio rice and finished with chunks of Dolcelatte cheese. I get everyone to do a 'shift' at the hob stirring when I do this one for friends.

Whiting with shrimp butter 26

Pan-fry chunky whiting fillets in butter. Finish with a good squeeze of lemon, a tub of brown shrimps and plenty of curly parsley. Great with oven chips and a dollop of tartare sauce. (The frozen chips act as an ice pack too.)

Mascarpone and rocket penne ⓥ 28

A fantastically fast sauce . . . Warm a bashed garlic clove or two in olive oil. Stir in mascarpone, Parmesan and rocket and warm through until wilted. Stir in hot penne and serve.

Sticky mango chicken salad 31

Chunks of chicken thigh marinated in mango chutney, garlic, lime juice and cumin. Stir-fry and serve with fresh leaves, mango and cucumber.

Tomato and Taleggio tart ⓥ 32

Just three ingredients to make this fantastic tart – ready-rolled puff pastry, mixed tomatoes and chunks of Taleggio. Bake and serve with salad.

Ever-ready lamb curry 35

A rich aromatic lamb curry cooked in coconut milk. Definitely a make-and-take dish that will happily sit on the hob for any latecomers. To serve, pop some fresh spinach and coriander in the bottom of a bowl and ladle the curry over.

Parma and mozzarella melts 36

Wrap halved chunks of mozzarella and some fresh basil leaves with Parma ham. Pan-fry until the mozzarella starts to ooze. Serve with a lovely big salad and lots of fresh bread.

Teriyaki steaks with pak choi and noodles 39

Thick steaks pan-fried until medium rare, served on top of wilted pak choi flavoured with soy and ginger.

Sausage and porcini *ragù* with gnocchi

Serves 4 / Ready in 35 minutes

25g dried porcini mushrooms

400g great-quality sausages

3 garlic cloves, chopped

1 tablespoon chopped fresh rosemary

350g jar tomato and basil pasta sauce

75g small black olives, drained

500g ready-made fresh gnocchi

50g shaved Parmesan, to serve

A fantastically rich, warming Italian ragù that's also good over hot pasta such as tagliatelle.

Place the porcini mushrooms in a small bowl, pour over 150ml boiling water and set aside. Squeeze the sausages out of their skins into a bowl and discard the skins. Heat a large non-stick frying pan and add the sausagemeat. Break up the meat with a wooden spoon to a lovely rough texture. Cook over a medium heat for 5 minutes until browned.

Blot off any excess fat with a little kitchen roll before adding the garlic and rosemary. Cook for a further 2 minutes until fragrant. Drain the mushrooms, reserving the soaking liquid, and add to the pan along with the pasta sauce. Add the soaking liquid, taking care to leave any grit behind in the jug. Add the olives, bring to a gentle boil and then simmer for 15 minutes until perfectly rich.

Meanwhile, cook the gnocchi according to the pack instructions and drain well. Divide among 4 warmed shallow bowls, spoon the hot sauce over and top with the Parmesan and a little extra fresh rosemary.

Make & take ...

This sauce is all the better for being made the day before as the flavours will really develop overnight. Simply chill, double-bag in roomy food bags and pack into the cool box along with the gnocchi and Parmesan.

'I have absolutely no hesitation in using ready-made pasta sauces as so many of them are really great quality now. It's just a question of trying them out and finding your own favourites. Keep an eye on the seasoning as many of them are pretty well seasoned and really don't need anything else adding.'

Hot-smoked salmon fishcakes with dill and lemon sauce

400g lightly smoked salmon fillets

550g floury potatoes, peeled and cubed

1 bunch spring onions, chopped

4 tablespoons chopped fresh curly parsley

finely grated zest of 1 lemon

2 eggs, beaten

100g fresh white breadcrumbs

sunflower oil, for frying

for the sauce

150g pot soured cream

3 tablespoons chopped fresh dill

a squeeze of lemon, plus wedges for serving

Lightly smoked fresh salmon is available in most good supermarkets now and has a wonderfully subtle smoke flavour. If you can't find it, simply use natural fillets and stir in some chopped smoked salmon instead.

Preheat the oven to gas 6/200°C/180°C fan. Place the salmon fillets on a baking sheet and roast in the oven for 10–15 minutes until cooked through and lightly charred. Set aside to cool. Quickly combine the soured cream, dill and lemon juice. Season to taste and chill.

Meanwhile, cook the potatoes until tender. Drain well, return to the pan and heat gently to cook off any excess moisture. Tip into a roomy bowl and mash. Add the spring onions, parsley and lemon zest. Flake the fish over the potatoes, keeping it nice and chunky. Season with plenty of black pepper, combine and taste to see if it needs salt – smoked fish can be pretty salty, so watch out.

Shape the mixture into 12 rough cakes (they really don't have to be perfect!), place on a plate and chill for 15 minutes. Place the eggs in one shallow dish and the breadcrumbs in another. Dip the cakes into the egg and then coat in the breadcrumbs.

Heat a centimetre or so of oil in a large non-stick frying pan and add the fishcakes four at a time. Cook for about 3 minutes on each side until golden and piping hot. Serve with lemon wedges, a fresh cucumber and tomato salad and a good dollop of the dill and lemon sauce.

Make & take ...

These fishcakes can be made a week or so ahead, frozen and packed in food bags and then a cool bag for the journey. Place them on a couple of large plates to defrost thoroughly before frying.

'The trick to a great fishcake is texture and seasoning. All that bland potato needs a bit of livening up, so pile on the flavour and taste the raw mix before you shape them. Ensure you cook all the moisture out of the drained potatoes by returning them to the pan for a couple of minutes to help them stay nice and firm.'

Dolcelatte and leek risotto

Serves 4 / Ready in about 35 minutes

Ingredients

50g butter

2 medium leeks, halved and sliced

2 garlic cloves, finely chopped

300g Arborio risotto rice

200ml white wine

1 litre hot light vegetable stock

3 tablespoons chopped fresh flat-leaf parsley

150g Dolcelatte cheese, roughly chopped

I get everyone to do a shift at the hob, stirring, when I do this one for friends. If you place a wooden spoon in one hand and a glass of wine in the other, pretty much anyone is keen to have a go . . .

Melt the butter in a large, shallow pan or frying pan. Add the leeks and gently cook for 10 minutes until softened but not coloured. Add the garlic and cook for a further 2 minutes. Stir in the rice until coated in the buttery mixture and then pour in the wine. Bubble rapidly for a minute or so.

Add the stock a ladleful at a time, gently simmering and stirring as you go. Keep going for just under 20 minutes, until the rice is cooked and creamy with just a little bite. If you start to run out of stock, resort to freshly boiled water from the kettle.

Once cooked, pop a lid on and let it stand for a minute. When you're ready to serve, scatter with the parsley and carefully stir in the cheese. Spoon into warmed bowls.

Kids
You know yourself whether your kids will enjoy the flavour of blue cheese. If they're likely to resist, simply spoon theirs into bowls and top with finely grated Parmesan or Cheddar before adding the Dolcelatte to the rest.

'This risotto recipe really is a great basic worth getting to grips with. Once you've mastered it, adapt and change it as much as you like. Start by replacing the leek with diced squash and stir in a mound of Parmesan at the end of cooking. Or use a combination of chopped fresh mushrooms and a handful of rehydrated porcini for a risotto with bags of flavour. Stir in a dollop of mascarpone and a handful of Parmesan just before serving.'

Whiting with shrimp butter

Serves 4 / Ready in about 35 minutes

4 × 200g fillets
whiting, skin on

1 teaspoon Maldon
salt, crushed

2 tablespoons olive oil

for the shrimp butter

100g unsalted
butter, cubed

200g peeled
brown shrimp

finely pared zest
of 1 lemon plus a
squeeze of juice

3 tablespoons chopped
curly parsley

to serve

frozen oven chips

salad

lemon wedges

Friday night is fish-and-chips night, so if you fancy something just that little bit different, give this a try. You could go all out and make home-made chips, but why go to all that effort when you can buy really decent frozen oven chips – they make the perfect ice pack for transporting the rest of the ingredients, too . . .

Place the whiting on a large plate and scatter with the salt. Pop in the fridge, uncovered, for 30 minutes or as long as you've got – the salt draws out the moisture from the fish and really helps to firm it up. Blot the fish dry with some kitchen roll and remove a bit of the salt. Drizzle the fish with the oil and season with plenty of black pepper.

Heat two non-stick frying pans until really hot and add two pieces of fish to each. Cook over a high heat for 2–3 minutes each side. Reduce the heat a little and dot over the butter. Add the shrimp and lemon zest as soon as the butter starts to foam and then squeeze over some lemon juice.

Cook for a couple of minutes, shaking the pan occasionally so that all the shrimps are coated in hot butter. Check the seasoning and then scatter over the parsley. Serve on hot plates with chips, a handful of salad and some lemon wedges.

Brown shrimp
If you've never laid your hands on these tiny brown shrimp before, you're in for a shock – they're so moreish and so delicious, you may never seek out a tiger prawn again! If you can't find them, simply replace with the same quantity of halved cooked prawns.

'Whiting is part of the cod and pollack family and is in far less danger of overfishing than its cousins. Salting beforehand helps firm the flesh a little as well as adding a bit of extra flavour. If you can't get your hands on any whiting, simply use another firm-fleshed white fish instead – your fishmonger will be able to guide you.'

Mascarpone and rocket penne

350g penne

3 tablespoons olive oil

3 garlic cloves, bashed

150g mascarpone cheese

50g rocket

50g Parmesan, finely grated

By the time the pasta has cooked in the pan, the sauce should be ready – just the thing for exhausted travellers!

Cook the penne according to the pack instructions until *al dente*. Drain well, reserving some of the hot cooking liquid.

Pour the olive oil into a roomy pan, add the garlic cloves and very gently heat to infuse the oil with plenty of flavour. Remove and discard the garlic and stir the mascarpone cheese into the oil. Heat through without boiling and season very well.

Tip the hot pasta into the pan and gently turn with a wooden spoon to coat in the sauce. Add a splash of the reserved cooking liquid if it needs a little extra help to coat. Add the rocket and gently stir through. Spoon into warmed bowls and scatter with the Parmesan.

It's annoying, I know . . .
I've used just 150g from a 200g pot of mascarpone cheese – you could use the whole pot if you fancy, but it is pretty rich. Keep the remainder and whisk it into eggs for really rich scrambled eggs or swirl into hot soup to add a wonderful velvety texture.

'This fantastic recipe requires very few ingredients for a great-tasting result. In fact, I'm sure it's one of those recipes that I invented on coming face to face with an empty fridge. If you like, you could add a handful of basil leaves to the finished thing or scatter over some crisp fried pancetta for a bit of oomph . . .'

Sticky mango chicken salad

Serves 4 / Ready in 25 minutes

600g skinless, boneless
chicken thighs

1 tablespoon
sunflower oil

for the marinade

3 tablespoons good-
quality mango chutney

½ small ripe mango,
stoned, peeled and diced

1½ teaspoons cumin
seeds, lightly crushed

4 garlic cloves, chopped

4 tablespoons fresh
coriander, roughly chopped

3 tablespoons lime juice

1 tablespoon olive oil

to serve

crisp salad leaves

1 mango, stoned, peeled
and roughly chopped

½ cucumber,
roughly chopped

1 bunch spring
onions, sliced

lime wedges and
more fresh coriander

I just love this flavour combination – sweet sticky chicken with zesty lime and plenty of garlic. Perfect with a cool, crisp salad.

Cut the chicken thighs into large chunks and place in a non-metallic bowl. Combine the marinade ingredients and season well. Spoon over the chicken and stir well to combine. Allow to marinate for 15 minutes.

Heat the sunflower oil in a wok or large non-stick frying pan and add the chicken. Stir-fry over a medium-high heat for about 10 minutes until cooked through and lightly charred.

To serve, arrange the salad leaves in a serving dish and top with the chicken, mango, cucumber and spring onion. Add some lime wedges and garnish with fresh coriander. Serve straight away.

Tip

Once cooked, allow the chicken to rest in a bowl for just a few minutes before serving. It'll be way more tender, plus it won't be such a shock for the cool crisp leaves when you come to putting the whole thing together.

'OK, they are slightly more calorific than lean white breast meat, but for me thighs win hands down (or is that feet down?). Packed with flavour and wonderfully juicy, they are far less likely to dry out after a blast in the wok or under a hot grill.'

Tomato and Taleggio tart

Serves 4 / Ready in 25 minutes

375g pack ready-made, ready-rolled puff pastry

650g mixed fresh tomatoes (I went for 1 beef tomato, halved and thickly sliced, 2 plum tomatoes, cut into thick wedges and 150g baby plum tomatoes)

1 tablespoon olive oil

200g Taleggio cheese, cubed

Just three basic ingredients are needed to make this fantastically easy tart. Serve very simply with a few rocket leaves and a glass of chilled wine.

Preheat the oven to gas 7/220°C/200°C fan. Allow the pastry to come up to room temperature a little before unrolling. Find your largest flat baking sheet and roll the pastry out so it fits it pretty much perfectly. Carefully lift on to the baking sheet.

Score a 3cm rim all around the pastry and arrange the tomatoes over the pastry within this area. Drizzle with the oil and season with plenty of black pepper. Bake for 5 minutes. Scatter over the cheese and then return to the oven for a further 5–10 minutes until golden and bubbling. Slice and serve.

Tip
If you find your holiday cottage is short on rolling pins, just use a chilled bottle of wine instead.

'The Taleggio in this tart melts to a delicious, unctuous mass that definitely benefits from sitting for a minute or so before slicing. If you've not been able to get your hands on any Taleggio, go for a wedge of full-flavoured, ripe Brie instead.'

Ever-ready lamb curry

Serves 4 very generously / Ready in 2 hours, 30 minutes

3 tablespoons
sunflower oil

1½kg neck of lamb, cut
into large chunks

2 onions, sliced

10 garlic cloves, chopped

1 tablespoon chopped
fresh ginger

15 curry leaves

2 cinnamon sticks

3–5 dried red chillies
(depending on how hot
you like it)

10 cardamom pods

3 teaspoons cumin seeds

2 teaspoons fennel seeds

2 teaspoons ground
turmeric

400ml can coconut milk

300ml light chicken stock

2 × 400g cans chickpeas,
drained and rinsed

6 tablespoons chopped
fresh coriander

150g fresh baby leaf
spinach

A great make-and-take dish for your first night on holiday. This is one of my old fail-safe curries that will quite happily sit on the hob simmering away for any late arrivals.

Heat half the oil in a large non-stick frying pan. Add the lamb and cook over a medium-high heat until well browned – you'll need to do this in batches. Remove each batch with a slotted spoon and place in a large pan. Cook the onion along with a good teaspoon of salt in the frying pan with the remainder of the oil. Cook for 10–15 minutes until perfectly tender and just beginning to colour.

Add the garlic, ginger, curry leaves and all the spices except the turmeric and cook for a further 2–3 minutes until fragrant. Add the turmeric and cook for 1 minute. Stir in the coconut milk and chicken stock and then pour over the lamb in the big pan.

Bring almost to the boil, cover and simmer for 1 hour, 30 minutes. Stir in the chickpeas and simmer for 30 minutes. At this point the curry can be served, chilled and stored, or chilled and frozen. If you're ready to eat, check the seasoning. Place some coriander and a handful of spinach leaves in each bowl and ladle the curry on top. Serve with poppadoms, mango chutney and all your favourite curry 'trimmings'.

Tip

I prefer to go for bone-in neck of lamb when I'm making a really slow-cooked curry as I think the bones add so much flavour. It's also a good excuse to eat with your fingers. If you prefer, you could replace with just 1kg boneless neck of lamb.

'If you were to add the spinach to the pan and continue cooking for any length of time, you'd be faced with a pretty grey-looking curry. By placing the leaves in the serving bowls and just letting the heat of the curry wilt them, you know you're going to have a curry with plenty of colour and life.'

Parma and mozzarella melts

4 x 100g packs
mozzarella balls,
drained

16 slices Parma ham

a good handful
basil leaves

2 tablespoons olive oil

to serve

100g bag mixed
salad leaves

250g baby plum
tomatoes, halved

1–2 tablespoons
balsamic vinegar,
to glaze

fresh crusty bread

I'm a bit hard-pushed to remember a more simple, satisfying and slightly over-the-top supper than this. I could, unfortunately, eat quite a lot of this given half a chance.

Blot the mozzarella on kitchen paper to remove any excess moisture and tear each in half. Place a couple of slices of Parma ham on a chopping board so that they overlap slightly. Scatter with a few basil leaves and top with a piece of mozzarella. Add a good grind of black pepper.

Wrap the ham around the cheese to completely encase it. The ham should stay in place without the need for any cocktail sticks. Repeat with the remaining cheese to make 8 mozzarella parcels in total.

Heat the oil in a large non-stick frying pan and add half the parcels. Fry over a medium-high heat for 2–3 minutes, turning every now and then until crisp and beginning to ooze and give a little. Set aside and keep warm while you cook the remainder.

To serve, divide the salad and tomatoes among four plates, top each with two melts and drizzle with a little balsamic. Serve with lots of warm, crusty bread.

Tip
You can get ahead with these by wrapping the mozzarella balls an hour or so in advance, then just frying them at the last minute.

'Go for a salad bag full of crisp sturdy leaves for this one – anything too soft would wilt and die the moment the hot melts hit it.'

Teriyaki steaks with pak choi and noodles

Serves 4 / Ready in 15 minutes

4 × 250g thick
sirloin steaks

1½ tablespoons oil

250g fine egg noodles

6 spring onions,
finely shredded

8 heads baby pak choi

a good handful of fresh
coriander

for the dressing

juice of 2 limes

2 teaspoons grated
fresh ginger

1 large garlic
clove, crushed

1 red chilli, deseeded
and finely chopped

4 tablespoons soy sauce

1 tablespoon
brown sugar

2 tablespoons olive oil

The sweet saltiness of this dressing is the perfect foil for a big, thick wodge of steak. Utterly delicious served with crisp fresh-tasting pak choi and lots of hot egg noodles.

Combine all of the dressing ingredients and set to one side. Drizzle the steaks with 1 tablespoon of the oil and season well. Heat a heavy frying pan until searing hot and smoking (if you have two, all the better), add the steaks and cook for 2–3 minutes each side or until cooked as you like them.

Set the steaks aside on a warm plate to rest a while. Meanwhile cook the egg noodles according to the pack instructions and drain. Wipe the frying pan with kitchen roll, reheat and add the remaining oil. Add the spring onions, reserving a few for garnish. Add the pak choi and a splash of water and cook over a high heat for 2–3 minutes until just wilted.

To serve, divide the noodles between four warmed bowls and top with sliced steak and pak choi. Add some coriander and drizzle over the dressing. Serve straight away with some extra lime wedges and the reserved spring onions.

Tip
For the best results, always allow steaks to sit out of the fridge for a wee while before cooking and always, always allow to rest before serving. You'll be rewarded with tenderness beyond belief.

'If you're feeling particularly flush (or maybe you're just cooking for two), you could go for thick fillet steaks for this one. Cook as above, then slice thickly and lay on top of the pak choi and hot noodles before dressing.'

Breakfasts and brunch

I rarely go to town with breakfast during the week. It usually consists of a slice of toast, or I join the children in a bowl of porridge, with optional smiley face etched in jam on the top! But at the weekend that all changes, especially if we've got friends over or we're having a weekend away . . .

Porridge is happily replaced with roasted sausages and bacon butties – the only dilemma being 'Brown or red sauce?' Eggy bread is bound to make an appearance, especially if children are on the scene, not to mention fruit smoothies or dippy eggs with toast.

Take your pick from quick, light breakfasts for when you know lunch is just round the corner, or go for something more substantial if your next meal might not happen until much later on or you know you're going to expend a lot of energy during the day.

Whichever option you go for, I've tried my best to keep it simple. My 'full English' needs just one roasting tin for the sausages and bits, and one pan to poach, scramble or fry your eggs – much easier than juggling pans and monitoring grills first thing, plus the washing-up is halved.

There's a great savoury muffin recipe that you can make at home and wheel out on the day – delicious after a short spell in the oven. Or why not go for a ham and Gruyère melt with optional Bloody Mary? The perfect pick-me-up for the morning after.

Simple recipes to start the day

Blueberry and honey pancakes 45

Delicious light pancakes filled with blueberries cooked in honey and served with Greek yogurt. I've included jug measures here as most holiday cottages wouldn't have a set of scales but more than likely would have a measuring jug.

Honeyed citrus fruits with ricotta 46

Pink grapefruit, oranges and mandarins drizzled with orange-blossom honey and served with a spoonful of ricotta.

Soft-boiled eggs with chorizo crisps, asparagus and warm bread 49

Thinly sliced chorizo fried until crisp – perfect for dipping into soft-boiled eggs along with chunks of fresh warm bread.

Mango and lime not-quite-so-smoothie 50

Ripe mangoes, lime, yogurt and milk smushed together with a fork for a deliciously fresh-tasting not-quite-smooth smoothie. Great if you haven't got a blender to hand.

Eggy bread with crisp bacon and blistered tomatoes 53

Thick-cut bread dipped in seasoned egg and fried in butter. Serve with roasted vine tomatoes and crisp streaky bacon.

Ham and Gruyère melts 54

Thick chunks of ham and grated Gruyère sandwiched between two slices of bread. Butter the outside and wrap in greaseproof paper. Pop in the oven and bake until golden and melted.

Bacon and Cheddar muffins 57

Gorgeous warm, savoury muffins filled with chunks of bacon, pumpkin seeds, semi-dried tomato and Cheddar cheese. Perfect straight from the oven.

Smoked salmon and cream cheese omelette 58

Perfect fluffy omelette filled with torn watercress, smoked salmon and a dollop of cream cheese. Serve with rye toast.

Bircher muesli with sugared peaches 61

Oats, dried fruits, apples and seeds soaked overnight in apple juice. Serve with yogurt and peaches.

Tray-roast breakfast with poached eggs 64

Place the sausages, mushrooms and tomatoes in the same roasting tin, drizzle with olive oil and a little balsamic, scatter with fresh thyme and roast. Perfect with a poached egg and a slice of toast.

Blueberry and honey pancakes

Serves 4 / Ready in 10 minutes

100g plain flour

1 medium egg

200–250ml milk

1 teaspoon
sunflower oil, plus
extra for frying

for the filling

300g blueberries

3 tablespoons
runny honey

to serve

Greek yogurt

extra honey

A lovely fresh start to the day. Feel free to fill them with whatever you fancy or have to hand. Bananas and Nutella is just one of my guilty secrets!

Place the flour in a bowl, add the egg and all but 50ml of the milk and beat until smooth. The consistency of the batter should be like single cream – so add the remainder of the milk if you feel it needs it. Stir in the teaspoon of oil and a pinch of salt.

Heat a non-stick frying pan, add just a tiny drizzle of oil and spread around the pan with a piece of kitchen roll. Add a little of the batter and swirl around the pan to make a thin pancake.

Cook for 2 minutes, turn and cook for another minute. Place on a plate, cover with a clean tea towel and keep warm in a very low oven whilst you make the remainder.

To make the filling, tip the blueberries into a pan and drizzle with the honey. Gently heat until just bursting and bubbling. To serve, place a couple of pancakes on each warmed serving plate, spoon over a little filling and fold into quarters. Serve with the yogurt and extra honey.

Tip

If you find yourself in a holiday cottage without any scales, you can still give these pancakes a go. 100g of flour is the equivalent of 150ml volume in a measuring jug. Just spoon in but don't pack down in order to get the right amount.

'I have no idea why it is, but without fail my first pancake to hit the pan is always a misshapen flop. It could be to do with the temperature of the pan (not hot enough), it could be to do with the oil (too much) or it could just be that I secretly want the first pancake of the day to be all mine ...'

Honeyed citrus fruits
with ricotta

Serves 4 / Ready in 10 minutes

*3 oranges, rind cut
off and sliced*

*2 pink grapefruit, rind
cut off and segmented*

*2 clementines, peeled
and segmented*

*4–6 tablespoons
runny honey*

*250g pot
ricotta cheese*

*Cool, clean, refreshing flavours that will leave you
with a wonderful vitamin-C tingle all morning. Use
whichever citrus fruits you prefer and can get hold of.*

Divide the citrus fruit between four shallow bowls
and drizzle each with some honey. Add a decent-sized
spoonful of ricotta to each and serve.
    Perfect served with fresh mint tea.

Tip

If you haven't got any ricotta cheese, this breakfast will taste just as lovely with
a good dollop of cool, creamy Greek yogurt.

*'If you're lucky enough to find fresh mint in the garden, or you were clever enough
to remember to bring some along, try making your own mint tea. Simply place a
handful of torn leaves in a warmed teapot and pour over freshly boiled water.
Serve as is or pep up with lemon and honey.'*

Soft-boiled eggs with chorizo crisps, asparagus and warm bread

Serves 4 / Ready in 10 minutes

8 eggs

2 × 110g packs chorizo sausage, sliced

200g asparagus, trimmed

crusty bread, warmed in the oven

I just love the big, bold taste of hot, crisp chorizo sausage dipped into a perfectly cooked boiled egg.

Bring a pan of water to the boil and very gently lower in the eggs. Cook for 2–3 minutes, depending on how you like them, and transfer to four serving plates.

Meanwhile, heat a large frying pan until hot and add the chorizo. Cook for 5 minutes until crisp and lightly charred.

Steam the asparagus for 2 minutes or until tender and serve with the eggs, chorizo and bread.

Tip

There's no way I'm about to tell you how to boil an egg – everybody's method and timing is different. Just don't use eggs straight from the fridge – they'll probably crack in the water – and use a timer. (I never do, I get distracted and my eggs are almost always that bit too hard!)

'Other great things to dip into soft-boiled eggs have to include the obvious hot toast with a huge payload of salty butter, or how about thick flakes of hot smoked salmon with some toasted rye?'

Mango and lime not-quite-so smoothie

2 ripe mangoes, stoned, peeled and chopped

a good squeeze of lime

8 tablespoons Greek yogurt

300ml milk

If you haven't got a blender to hand, you can still whip up smoothies for a really refreshing breakfast. The only rule is to make sure you use really ripe soft fruit and put a bit of work into smushing the flesh with a fork.

Place the mango flesh in a bowl and mash as much as you can to a smooth purée. Tip into a large jug, add a good squeeze of lime and then stir in the remaining ingredients. Have a little taste and add more lime if you like. Pour into chunky glasses and serve.

Tip
Lots of different soft fruits can be made into a really delicious smoothie … Raspberries and bananas are great, as are strawberries and banana with a squeeze of fresh orange. If you want to make them a little more substantial to tide you over until lunch, stir in a spoonful of oats.

'Always on the lookout for a nice little cocktail idea, I've used this basic squashing of ripe fruit as the basis of many a fantastic cocktail! Try squashed mango, add plenty of ice, a shot of Malibu, a squeeze of lime and a splash of soda – oh, and a very thick straw to avoid mango blockages!'

Eggy bread with crisp bacon and blistered tomatoes

Serves 4 / Ready in 25 minutes

750g cherry
vine tomatoes

2 tablespoons olive oil

6 eggs

8 medium slices white
bloomer bread

50g butter

8 rashers smoked
streaky bacon

A wonderful breakfast dish that the whole family will love. If there are any veggies with you, this is also delicious with roasted mushrooms.

Preheat the oven to gas 6/200°C/180°C fan and preheat the grill to high. Place the tomatoes in a roasting tin, drizzle with the oil and season well. Roast for 15–20 minutes until softened and blistered. Beat the eggs in a roomy bowl and season well. Dip in a couple of slices of bread.

Heat some of the butter in a large non-stick frying pan until foaming (if you've got two pans, all the better!) and add 2–3 slices of the dipped bread. Cook over a medium-high heat for about 4 minutes until golden. Flip over and cook the other side for 2–3 minutes. Keep warm whilst you dip and cook the remainder.

Meanwhile, cook the bacon under the preheated grill for just under 10 minutes. When you're ready to serve, place two slices of eggy bread on each warmed plate and top with the blistered tomatoes and crisp bacon. Fantastic served with chilli sauce or tomato ketchup.

Tip

Let the bread soak up some of the egg mixture and actually get quite soggy – the end result will be much nicer, with a lovely soft texture inside and a little bit of bite on the outside.

'Being more of a savoury person, I've never really got to grips with that whole honey-on-eggy-bread thing, but if you do find yourself hankering after something sweet one morning, this could be the way forward . . .'

Ham and Gruyère melts

Serves 4 / Ready in 25 minutes

200g thick-cut ham,
roughly sliced

8 thick hand-cut
slices white bread

100g Gruyère
cheese, grated

50g butter

to serve

tomato chutney

a large Bloody
Mary for anyone
who needs it

A great breakfast for a group of friends who are likely to make sporadic appearances at the breakfast table. Simply make them up, wrap in parchment and bake them as people emerge.

Preheat the oven to gas 6/200°C/180°C fan. Cut out 4 large squares of baking parchment and set to one side. Divide the ham between 4 slices of bread and top each with some of the cheese. Top with a slice of bread.

Place each sandwich on a piece of parchment and butter the outside (top and bottom). Wrap in the parchment so they're completely encased. When you're ready to go, place on a baking sheet and bake in the oven for 20 minutes until golden and bubbling. Serve straight away with a spoonful of chutney and optional Bloody Mary.

Hair of the dog

If you fancy a real pick-me-up, give this a go . . . Mix a pint of tomato juice, 200ml vodka, a good nip of celery salt, a glug of Worcestershire sauce, plenty of leafy celery stalks, to stir, and lots of ice in a jug. Stir in 2 tablespoons grated fresh horseradish from a jar for a real kick.

'For this, shop-bought wafer-thin ham just won't cut it! I know it sounds a bit heavy duty, but I really do like to take a big joint of home-cooked ham away with me. It's great not only for this breakfast but for sandwiches, pasta sauces or soups (see page 89 for a fantastic ham and lentil soup). But if this seems like a step too far, buy it thickly cut off the bone from the deli counter.'

Bacon and Cheddar muffins

Makes 8 muffins / Ready in 30 minutes

125g streaky
bacon, chopped

150g mushrooms,
chopped

225g plain flour

1 teaspoon
baking powder

4 tablespoons chopped
flat-leaf parsley

100g Cheddar cheese,
finely grated

175ml milk

1 egg, beaten

100g butter, melted

I love making muffins as there's absolutely no talent, elbow grease or tricky techniques required. It's just a case of adding the wet ingredients to the dry and keeping the batter lumpy.

Preheat the oven to gas 6/200°C/180°C fan and line a muffin tin with 8 cases. Heat a frying pan until pretty hot and add the bacon and mushrooms. Cook for 5–6 minutes until golden and all the liquid has cooked off the mushrooms. Allow to cool a little before placing in a large mixing bowl.

Add the flour, baking powder, parsley and half the cheese and combine well. Beat together the milk, egg and butter and add to the flour mixture. Stir to combine but don't be tempted to overwork as a few lumps here and there make for a better batter.

Spoon into the prepared muffin tin and scatter over the remaining cheese. Bake for 15–20 minutes until risen and golden. Turn out and stand for 15 minutes before devouring.

Make & take . . .
Either make the day before, cool and then store in an airtight container, or make well in advance and freeze and allow to defrost overnight. Either way, give these muffins a little pep-up in a warm oven just before serving.

'These delicious muffins are great eaten as they are, or halve and butter them and serve with cherry tomatoes and creamy scrambled egg. If you have any left over, take them with you for a quick snack for the kids later on in the day.'

Smoked salmon and cream cheese omelette

Makes 2 omelettes / Ready in 10 minutes

4 eggs, beaten

1 tablespoon chopped
fresh chives

1 tablespoon butter

for the filling

50g light cream cheese

100g smoked
salmon, sliced

a good handful of
watercress leaves

You need to be in a very generous mood to make these for any kind of a gathering as they need to be made individually and 'to order', if you see what I mean. Maybe set aside this recipe for just the two of you . . .

Beat the eggs and chives together and season well. Heat a small non-stick frying pan until searing hot, add half the butter and swirl straight away as it foams and bubbles. Immediately add half the egg mixture and cook over a very high heat, whisking for a minute until it begins to firm up.

Allow to cook for 1–2 minutes, depending on how set you like your omelettes. Add a good splodge of cream cheese to one half, top with half the salmon and half the watercress. Flip over and slide on to a warmed plate. Serve straight away with hot toast while you cook the other one.

Tip
The trick to a great omelette is to have a really good non-stick pan and heat it well so that the butter foams and jumps around in the pan as soon as it hits it. I always slightly under-do the eggs as I know it will keep on cooking once filled and folded.

'Once you've mastered the art of the perfect omelette – slightly creamy and runny on the inside and set on the outside – there's no limit to the amount of fillings you can add. Grated Cheddar, finely sliced red onion, coriander and a dangerous amount of jalapeño peppers is well worth a go.'

Bircher muesli with sugared peaches

Serves 4 / Ready in 5 minutes

150g oats

75g dried cherries

50g hazelnuts, chopped

2 tablespoons pumpkin seeds

2 tablespoons sunflower seeds

500ml apple juice

1 apple, peeled and coarsely grated

to serve

100–150ml milk

150g Greek yogurt

2 peaches, halved, stoned and sliced

100g blackberries

1 tablespoon brown sugar

A fantastically satisfying start to the day, with absolutely none of the guilt associated with most breakfasts this filling.

Combine all of the dried ingredients in a roomy bowl. Pour over the apple juice and stir in the grated apple. Cover with cling film and chill overnight in the fridge.

To serve, spoon into bowls and add enough milk to give a nice creamy consistency. Top with the yogurt, peaches and blackberries and sprinkle with the sugar.

Make & take . . .

You could make the dry mix up at home and pop it into a food bag, then simply add the apple juice and grated apple the night before you want to eat it – in which case, it's well worth making double the quantity.

'Go for whatever fruit you fancy on top of this lovely muesli. Banana and blueberries, cherries and apricots – it really is fantastically adaptable.'

Tray-roast breakfast with poached eggs

12 chipolata sausages

8 Portobello mushrooms

12 medium vine tomatoes

2 sprigs thyme

1 tablespoon balsamic vinegar

2 tablespoons olive oil

to serve

8 eggs

lots of hot buttered toast

A fantastically simple way of cooking everyone's favourite breakfast.

Preheat the oven to gas 6/200°C/180°C fan. Place the sausages in a large roasting tin and cook for 15 minutes. Turn and then add the mushrooms and tomatoes to the same tin. Tuck the thyme in under the mushrooms and tomatoes and drizzle with the balsamic and oil.

Return to the oven for a further 15–20 minutes until everything is looking pretty much done. Meanwhile, poach the eggs and make plenty of toast. Divide among four warmed plates and serve.

Tip
If you go for fat sausages instead of chipolatas, cook them for an additional 10 minutes before adding the mushrooms and tomatoes.

'Juggling lots of pots and pans really is no fun first thing, plus it creates a huge amount of washing-up. The only thing you won't get away with roasting in the tin is bacon – so if you do fancy a rasher or two, you will need to put the grill on.'

Easy lunches

Whether you intend to head outdoors for lunch or snuggle up for a lazy afternoon inside, I think it's always best to keep lunch quite simple. Pretty much all of the lunches that follow are one-bowl or one-plate affairs that are highly transportable, whether it's to the lawn, a rickety old table outside or maybe even the beach.

The few exceptions include the Mexican quesadillas that just cry out for extra bowls of salsa, guacamole, soured cream and chillis, and the warming ham and lentil soup – unless of course you're feeling brave enough to pop it into a big old Thermos flask and head out to the beach with a blanket and some bread!

Whichever you choose, be guided by the time of year and what's at its absolute best and in season. The summer-vegetable salad with Parma ham is one of my favourites as it's just so easy to make and is packed with all the great flavours that summer has to offer.

If it's summer and there's a beach near by, I'd always be tempted to plump for the seared mackerel with fennel salad, especially if there's any chance of trying to catch my own. That said, whenever we go out to catch our own lunch (or tea), my husband always puts the same contingency plan in place: take some sossies for the barbie just in case your luck's out! Needless to say, we eat a lot of sausages . . .

Great recipes for relaxed lunches

Summer salad with Parma ham 70

Asparagus, fresh broad beans, sugar snaps and peas steamed until perfectly tender, topped with Parma ham and a drizzle of fruity olive oil. Serve with fresh (bought!) mayo flavoured with fresh herbs, lemon juice and garlic.

Home-made burgers with salsa and soured cream 73

Burgers flavoured with fresh coriander, garlic, red onion and tomato ketchup (yes, I know it sounds strange, but the sweetness of the sauce really does work!) Grill and serve with bought salsa pepped up with a handful of fresh coriander and a spoonful of soured cream.

Camembert melts with orchard fruits ⓥ 74

Boxes of Camembert wrapped in foil and baked until oozing. Serve with ripe fruits, plenty of fresh bread and a big glass of red wine.

Seared mackerel with fennel salad and picnic bread 79–80

The perfect beach lunch cooked on a disposable barbie. Add a squeeze of lemon and serve with a salad of thinly sliced raw fennel combined with orange segments, fresh herbs and black olives.

Mussels in coconut broth 83

A simple coconut broth flavoured with lemongrass, ginger, garlic and chilli. Simmer and drop in the mussels. Cook for a few moments, scatter with lots of fresh coriander and serve straight away.

Quesadillas with guacamole and pinto-bean salsa ⓥ 84–7

Soft flour tortillas filled with cheese, spring onions, jalapeños, avocado and tomato. Fry in a smidge of oil until crisp and oozing. Serve with guacamole and a simple pinto-bean salsa.

Ham and lentil soup 89

Thick chunks of ham cooked with onion, potato and lentils. Simmer and serve with home-made herb croutons.

Panzanella with griddled halloumi ⓥ 90

A delicious garlicky, oily salad of bread, tomatoes, cucumber, red onion and olives topped with hot griddled halloumi and an extra squeeze of lemon.

Hot chicken doorstep with Dijon mayo 93

Tender chicken thighs marinated in lemon, olive oil and thyme. Grill, then top with Gruyère. Sandwich in toasted thick bread with rocket, beef tomatoes and a good dollop of Dijon mayonnaise.

Lamb with Kalamata marinade 94

Roughly chop Kalamata olives and semi-dried tomatoes; combine with fresh oregano, garlic and olive oil and spread over lamb cutlets, chops or leg steaks. Barbecue or grill and serve with warm flatbread and a crisp salad.

Summer salad
with Parma ham

Serves 4 / Ready in 15 minutes

300g broad beans

300g asparagus

150g fresh peas
(defrosted if frozen)

225g sugar snaps

2 × 88g packs
Parma ham, torn

2 tablespoons olive oil

for the garlic mayo

190g pot fresh
mayonnaise

a squeeze of
fresh lemon

1 tablespoon finely
chopped chives

1 tablespoon finely
chopped parsley

1 garlic clove, crushed

A fantastically light summer lunch that needs nothing much more than maybe a wedge of bread and a glass of chilled rosé.

Bring a big pot of water to the boil and drop in the broad beans. Cook for 2 minutes then scoop out and refresh under cold water. Peel the larger ones and leave the skin on any of the smaller ones. Place in a big bowl.

Add the asparagus and peas to the boiling water and cook for 2 minutes. Add the sugar snaps and cook for just one minute more. Drain and refresh under cold water and blot dry with kitchen roll. Add to the broad beans and combine.

To make the garlic mayo, stir everything together and season with black pepper and maybe a tiny bit of salt. Divide the veg among four serving plates and scatter over the Parma ham. Drizzle with the oil and serve with a good splodge of the garlic mayo.

Tip
You really can go for whatever delicate summer vegetables you fancy. Aim for around 900g in total weight and just be guided by what looks great at the greengrocers.

'You could make your own mayonnaise, but you are on holiday after all! Hunt out ready-made fresh mayonnaise from supermarkets and delis. They're fantastically rich and creamy, but more importantly they'll save you a lot of time and arm ache!'

Home-made burgers with salsa and soured cream

Serves 4 / Ready in 30 minutes

500g mince (not too lean!)

125g chorizo, finely chopped

1 red onion, finely chopped

1 fat garlic clove, crushed

2 tablespoons tomato sauce

4 tablespoons chopped
fresh coriander

1 egg yolk

to serve

150g pot fresh salsa

2 tablespoons
sweet chilli sauce

4 crusty rolls,
split and toasted

4–5 tablespoons
soured cream

cos lettuce,
leaves separated

1 avocado, sliced

1 small red onion,
finely sliced

jalapeño peppers,
as many as you like

I remember serving one of these up to a friend who'd never had a burger other than something served out of a fast-food carton. He nearly fell over backwards! So, if you've never been tempted before, give them a go – they're a cinch.

Place all the burger ingredients in a bowl and season well. Combine thoroughly – use your hands for this: it's so much easier. Shape into 8 fat burgers and set to one side until you need them. Pep up the bought salsa by stirring in the sweet chilli sauce and chill.

Cook the burgers under a medium grill for 15–20 minutes until seared and cooked through, turning as you go. You could cook them on a barbie if you fancied for about the same amount of time.

To serve, place the base of a roll on each plate and top with a burger. Spoon over the salsa and soured cream and serve garnished with any or all of the suggestions. Top each with a roll lid and serve.

Tip

Don't be tempted to use mince that's too lean when you're making burgers. You do need a bit of fat because it adds flavour and moistness as it cooks through – and a lot of it will cook out on a barbie or grill.

'I know it sounds a bit strange putting tomato ketchup in a burger mix, but it really does work – the sweetness of the sauce and the rich tomato flavour add another dimension. When you're cooking them, don't be tempted to shuffle and shove them around on the grill too much as they may break up. Instead, just let them cook through and "firm up" before turning.'

Camembert melts with orchard fruits

2 × 250g rounds of
boxed Camembert

6 ripe plums,
halved, stoned
and thickly sliced

300g black grapes

1 ripe pear,
thickly sliced

plenty of warm
crusty bread

This is a really lazy lunch that's perfect if all your other activities have been rained off for the afternoon. Even better if you're looking for an excuse to open that lovely big bottle of red . . .

Preheat the oven to gas 6/200°C/180°C fan. Take the cheese out of the box and remove any wax paper. Place the cheese back in the box and double-wrap in foil, remembering which is the right way up.

Bake the cheese for 15–20 minutes – you can kind of hear the cheese bubbling when it's ready if you listen carefully! Remove the lid and serve with the fruit and roughly torn bread.

Tip
You really could serve the Camembert with any fruits you fancy here: apples, ripe pears, soft sweet figs or stoned dates.

'This simple little dish can also be cooked over a barbie or just next to the embers of a wood fire if you've got one fired up.'

Seared mackerel with fennel salad

Serves 4 / Ready in 30 minutes

4 whole fresh
mackerel, cleaned

2 tablespoons olive oil

1 lemon, cut into
thick wedges

picnic bread, to serve
(see page 80)

for the salad

2 oranges

2 fennel bulbs,
halved and very
finely shredded

3 tablespoons olive oil

100g black olives

1 teaspoon white
wine vinegar

2 tablespoons
chopped chives

The ultimate simple beach-side lunch that tastes even better if you're lucky enough to catch it yourself.

Firstly, cut the peel off the orange with a sharp knife, making sure you get rid of all the pith too. Hold the orange over a bowl whilst you cut out the segments, leaving the membranes behind. Squeeze a little of the juice from the membrane into the bowl. Add the other salad ingredients, combine and season to taste. Chill until needed.

Drizzle the mackerel with the olive oil, squeeze over some of the lemon and season to taste. If you're cooking the mackerel on a barbecue, pop it on and cook it for about 5–10 minutes on each side, turning it only once. Serve straight from the grill with a good spoonful of the fennel salad and a chunk of picnic bread.

Cooking times

How long the mackerel takes to cook depends on the fierceness of your barbie and the thickness of your mackerel. Whatever you do, don't be tempted to keep flipping and turning or it will fall apart.

'Fennel has a real affinity with fish, so you could try this lovely fresh salad with any of your favourite fish dishes. It tastes pretty good with hot grilled chicken too.'

Picnic bread

Makes 3 small loaves / Ready in 30 minutes, plus rising time

500g pack white
bread mix (e.g.
Wright's Premium)

2 good sprigs of thyme

3 garlic cloves, sliced

3 tablespoons olive oil

I know I sound a bit mad, but I always take one of those ready-made bread mixes away with me just in case all that's available is claggy white sliced!

Make the bread mix up according to the pack instructions. Split into three and when you're ready to let it rise in its final shape, roll out and place in 3 × 20cm cake tins or disposable foil trays.

Preheat the oven to gas 6/200°C/180°C fan. Allow to rise as per the instructions and then indent each loaf with your fingers to create deep delves. Scatter with the thyme and garlic, drizzle with the oil and add a good scattering of sea salt. Bake for 10–15 minutes until golden.

Tip
If you haven't taken any plain flour to your holiday cottage, remember to keep back a little of the dry flour mix to help with kneading later on. I learned this trick the hard way and got into a right old sticky mess!

'Once you get into cooking up these fantastically quick bread mixes, there's no end to the amount of different ingredients and flavours you can pile on top. Try adding chopped semi-dried tomatoes, baby tomatoes, oil and rosemary or go for caramelized onions with lots of sharp Cheddar.'

Mussels in coconut broth

Serves 4 / Ready in 15 minutes

2 tablespoons
sunflower oil

1 bunch spring
onions, chopped

4 cloves garlic,
chopped

2 lemongrass stalks,
peeled, bashed and
finely chopped

4cm piece ginger,
finely chopped

1 red chilli, deseeded
and chopped

400ml can light
coconut milk

2kg live mussels

juice of 1 lime, plus
wedges to serve

1–2 tablespoons
fish sauce

6 tablespoons roughly
chopped coriander

If you do think ahead and have a chance to take all the fresh spices and herbs for this one, you'll be rewarded with a lunch that you'll want to cook over and over again. Oh, and I've gone for light coconut milk here as I always feel the full-fat version is just a little bit too rich for mussels.

Heat a wok or large frying pan until searing hot. Add the oil and swirl around. Add the spring onions, garlic, lemongrass, ginger and chilli and stir-fry for about 2 minutes until fragrant. Add the coconut milk, bring to the boil and then drop in the mussels.

Cover immediately and cook for about 4 minutes until they're all open. Add a good squeeze of lime and pour over the fish sauce to taste. Spoon into warmed bowls and serve scattered with the coriander and a couple of lime wedges.

Tip
If you haven't got fish sauce, it really doesn't matter. Instead, season with salt and add an extra squeeze of lime.

'I'm not quite sure why, but mussels seem to be a lot easier to prepare and clean than they used to be. If you do have any that come with frondy beards, simply pull them away. Likewise, if any of them are particularly covered in barnacles, just scrape them off with a small knife. The only other thing to do is give them a good rinse in cold tap water and throw away any that remain open or are cracked. Once you've finished cooking, look out for any that have stayed shut and, again, just chuck them away.'

Quesadillas with guacamole and pinto-bean salsa

8 soft flour tortillas

50g baby spinach

150g Cheddar cheese, grated

1 bunch spring onions, sliced

2 ripe avocados, thickly sliced

2 tomatoes, sliced

8 tablespoons roughly chopped coriander

jalapeño peppers, as many as you fancy

50g butter

The beauty of this lunch is that you can go as OTT with the fillings as you fancy. It's particularly good with crisp fried chorizo or grilled red peppers if you've got any knocking about in the fridge.

To make the quesadillas, place four flour tortillas on a work surface and divide the spinach among them. Top each with cheese and then the remaining ingredients equally. Add more jalapeños for anyone who likes spicy food. Finish each with a tortilla lid.

To cook, heat a non-stick frying pan until hot and add a knob of butter. Carefully place a quesadilla in the pan, trying not to let any filling spill out. Cook over a medium heat until crisp and golden – this should take 2–3 minutes. Carefully turn with the help of a spatula and a plate and cook on the other side. Repeat with the remaining quesadillas. Cut into wedges and serve.

Tip

If you want to get ahead with this lunch, fill the quesadillas and stack them on a couple of plates. Wrap in cling film to stop them drying out and then just cook when you're ready to go.

'Because you can only cook one or two quesadillas at a time, they absolutely have to be cut up and dished out on to a communal plate for sharing. If you do single plates for each person, some poor unfortunate is going to have to have a long wait!'

See page 86 for the salsa recipe and page 87 for the guacamole.

Pinto-bean salsa

Serves 4 / Ready in 10 minutes

2 fresh corn cobs, grilled until charred

400g can pinto beans, drained and rinsed

6 spring onions, sliced

4 tablespoons chopped coriander

1 small garlic clove, crushed

2 tablespoons olive oil

4 jalepeños, chopped

juice of 1 lime

I'm absolutely not talking home-cooked beans here: no way, you're on holiday! Just use canned ones and make sure you rinse them well before using.

Cut the corn from the cob with a sharp knife and place in a bowl. Add the remaining ingredients, adding just enough lime to taste. Season well, tasting as you go, and serve.

Tip
Grilling fresh corn until lightly charred gives it a wonderfully intense sweet flavour. If you haven't the time or inclination, just use 150g freshly cooked corn kernels instead.

'This salsa is delicious served with any Mexican meal – try it with chilli or spooned over grilled cheesy nachos.'

A great guacamole

Serves 4 / Ready in 5 minutes

3 ripe avocados,
halved and stoned

1 garlic clove, crushed

1 small red onion,
finely chopped

1 red chilli,
finely chopped

juice of 1 lime

For me, the trick to great guacamole is simply to keep tasting it and adding more seasoning and lime juice until the flavours just jump out.

Spoon the avocado flesh into a bowl and roughly mash with a fork. I prefer lots of texture, but do it how you like it. Add the remaining ingredients and keep seasoning and adding lime until it tastes fantastic!

Tip
If you make this in advance, spoon it into a bowl and cover the surface area with a disc of baking parchment or greaseproof paper to stop the air from getting to it and discolouring it.

'Go for the lovely dimply Hass avocados for this one as they taste so buttery and rich – the perfect foil for all those zesty, punchy flavours.'

Ham and lentil soup

Serves 4 / Ready in 35 minutes

2 tablespoons olive oil

1 large onion,
finely chopped

3 garlic cloves,
chopped

350g floury
potatoes, chopped

1 bay leaf, if you can
get your hands on it

150g red lentils

1 litre light stock

200g cooked ham,
roughly chopped

You know I was apologizing about how I sometimes take a piece of cooked ham when I go for a weekend away (see Ham and Gruyère melts, page 54)? Well, this is another reason why I take it – delicious home-cooked soup that takes absolutely no time to make.

Heat the oil in the largest saucepan you can find, add the onion and garlic and gently cook for 5 minutes. Add the potatoes and cook for another 2 minutes.

Add the bay leaf, lentils and stock and bring to the boil. Simmer for 20 minutes until the lentils are tender. Add the ham, plus a splash of boiling water if the soup seems a little too thick. Check the seasoning before ladling into warmed bowls.

If you have the time . . .
If you have a chunk of slightly stale bread going spare, try making your own croutons. Toss the cubed bread with a good glug of olive oil and season well. Add to a warm frying pan and cook until golden. Add extra flavour with torn thyme for the last minute of cooking.

'I love lentils. Whether they're red lentils, nutty brown ones or the utterly gorgeous black Puy lentils, I could eat them till the cows come home. Be sure to add plenty of flavour, season well and add a little drizzle of fruity olive oil to really give them a bit of oomph!'

Panzanella with griddled halloumi

Serves 4 / Ready in 15 minutes

125g stale bread, roughly torn

½ cucumber, roughly chopped

300g ripe tomatoes, cut into bite-sized chunks

1 small red onion, finely sliced

100g small black olives

good handful of flat-leaf parsley, roughly chopped

good handful of basil, roughly torn

for the dressing

1 tablespoon red wine vinegar

4–6 tablespoons olive oil

1 small garlic clove, crushed

½ teaspoon sugar

for the halloumi

1 tablespoon olive oil

250g pack halloumi, thinly sliced

1 bashed garlic clove

juice of ½ lemon

Unless you can get your hands on deliciously ripe British tomatoes, I would maybe give this recipe a wide berth as you really do need to rely on their luscious flavour. I usually go for a mixture of beef, vine and baby plum tomatoes for this one and then just cut them into manageable-sized chunks or wedges.

Place all of the panzanella ingredients in a big, roomy bowl and combine well. Whisk the dressing ingredients together and season very well. Drizzle over the panzanella, combine and set to one side. This is where you can add as much or as little of the oil as you fancy: your call!

To cook the halloumi, heat a non-stick frying pan and then drizzle in the oil. Add the halloumi and the bashed garlic clove and cook for 2–3 minutes on each side until golden brown. Season with black pepper (don't be tempted to add any salt) and squeeze over the lemon juice. To serve, pile the panzanella on to four plates and top with a few slices of halloumi.

Tip
If you haven't got any stale bread to hand, simply tear up fresh white bread and encourage it to dry out a little in a warm oven for 10 minutes or so.

'When you first look at an ingredient list this long, you might think "What a faff!", but there really couldn't be a simpler, more delicious lunch. Panzanella is absolutely addictive. I love it with barbecued chicken or very simply grilled fish.'

Hot chicken doorstep with Dijon mayo

Serves 4 / Ready in 20 minutes, plus marinating

6 skinless, boneless chicken thighs

2 tablespoons olive oil

juice of ½ lemon

a good few sprigs of thyme

8 thick hand-cut slices white bread, toasted

75g wild rocket

1 beef tomato, halved and sliced

75g Gruyère cheese, finely grated

for the Dijon mayo

8 tablespoons mayonnaise

1 tablespoon Dijon mustard

There's nothing quite like trying to take a dignified mouthful of sandwich when it's piled this high with goodies – you may want to eat it just with very good friends and keep a few napkins to hand!

Cut the chicken thighs into thick chunks and place in a bowl. Add the olive oil, lemon juice and strip the leaves from the thyme into the bowl. Season well and allow to marinate for 15 minutes or for as long as you've got.

Preheat the grill to medium and grill the chicken for 15 minutes, turning occasionally until cooked through and lightly charred. Meanwhile, combine the mayonnaise with the mustard and season to taste.

To make the sandwiches, place a slice of bread on each plate and spread with some mayo. Top with a handful of rocket, a few generous slices of tomato and then some of the hot chicken. Then add some of the Gruyère and try to balance the other slice of bread on top of that – a skewer may come in handy here. Serve as is or with a big bowl of chips.

Tip
We all tend to cook chicken to within an inch of its life and often the result is a horrid, chewy, dry offering. Instead, cook until just done and remember that the residual heat will keep it cooking as you put the sandwiches together.

'I'm definitely a thigh girl and not a breast girl, if you see what I mean. Yes, there is a little more fat involved, but for me the delicious tender texture of thigh far outweighs the few calories saved by opting for the dry, lacklustre taste of white meat.'

Lamb with Kalamata marinade

8–12 lamb cutlets,
depending on their size

2 tablespoons chopped
fresh rosemary

for the marinade

100g pitted Kalamata
olives, chopped

3 tablespoons olive oil

100g semi-dried
tomatoes, finely
chopped

2 garlic cloves,
chopped

1 tablespoon
balsamic glaze

2 tablespoons chopped
fresh parsley

to serve

2 red peppers

1/3 cucumber, chopped

pitta bread, warmed

lemon wedges

This involves a really simple salsa-come-marinade that you could make at home and then decant into a jar ready for your hols.

Combine all of the marinade ingredients and season well with black pepper – it shouldn't need any salt because of the olives. Place one-third in a food bag, drop the lamb cutlets into the bag, along with the rosemary, and allow to marinate for 15 minutes or so.

Cook the lamb cutlets on a barbecue (or grill) for 10–15 minutes, turning occasionally until cooked as you like them. At the same time, place the peppers on the barbie and keep turning until softened and lightly charred. Thickly slice and combine with the cucumber.

To serve, place the pitta bread on a plate, add some of the pepper and cucumber mix, top with 2–3 cutlets and spoon over some of the reserved salsa. Squeeze over a little lemon.

Tip

I love lamb cooked on a barbie, as it helps to cook out some of the fat. But watch out as it can cause the coals to flame and flare out of control. The answer is always to have a cup of water or water sprayer to hand to douse it down and prevent it getting too fierce.

You could of course substitute lamb chops for cutlets, or even leg steaks.

'For absolutely heaps of flavour, scatter fresh woody herbs over the coals as the lamb cooks. This smells divine and really does give a great flavour to the meat.'

Saturday night special

....

For me, Saturday night is all about bathing the kids that little bit earlier than usual and getting out the candles, polishing up any glassware you can find and pulling out all the stops for a really fun evening.

I don't think I'd ever be tempted to cook a three-course meal when I'm on holiday, though I'd definitely do two. But however many courses I decide to do, cooking something special doesn't mean spending hours and hours in the kitchen or presenting food that's been faffed and fiddled with. It's about choosing some lovely ingredients that I may not use every day (fresh local crab, for instance, or a fab cut of meat from the butcher's) and treating them very simply so that the ingredients can really shine.

I like the kind of food that involves people diving in and helping themselves, and for that reason I really do love putting together food that needs to be served on big communal platters. My tuna niçoise is exactly that and it's one of those gorgeous dishes that you can add to and change as much as you fancy and then just present very simply on the biggest platter you can find for everybody to help themselves.

For ease, the Chinese pork is a great little recipe to have up your sleeve – it's so easy to make and pretty much looks after itself in the oven whilst you get on with enjoying yourselves. I wheel this dish out about twice a year to friends who I know just love its melt-in-the-mouth texture and fabulous crackling.

Simple suppers for an evening of fun

Seafood linguine with coriander pesto 101

*Stir-fry spring onion, garlic and chilli with prawns and halved baby plum tomatoes.
Add a good squeeze of lime and stir in hot linguine and fresh crab meat. Serve with
a spoonful of home-made coriander pesto.*

Chinese belly pork with wilted spring greens 102

*Lean belly pork flavoured with Chinese five spice and garlic. Slow-roast until meltingly
tender, with fantastically crisp crackling. Serve with sticky rice and wilted greens.*

Marmalade-glazed sticky ribs 107

*Here, I've simmered racks of pork ribs in apple juice until tender – this also makes sure
they're completely cooked through before they even hit the barbecue. Marinate in a sticky
glaze of soy, marmalade, garlic and oil. Cook on the barbie until lightly charred and sticky.*

Garlicky prawn, clam and chorizo pot 110

*Slow-cooked onions, garlic and chorizo combined with peppers, chunks of waxy potatoes
and tomatoes. Top with huge prawns, simmer a little longer and serve with bread to
mop up the sauce.*

Vine tomato seared salmon with a lemon and herb dressing 113

*A whole side of wild salmon fast-roasted on a bed of vine tomatoes and lemon chunks.
Serve with a zesty herb dressing and buttered new potatoes.*

Aubergine steaks with pesto and griddled flatbreads Ⓥ 114

*Score thick aubergine steaks and drizzle with oil. Cook over a barbie until tender and
lightly charred. Spread with pesto and serve on hot flatbreads with plenty of Parmesan
and a crisp salad.*

Chicken in cider, garlic and tarragon sauce 119

*Part-boned chicken breasts pan-fried with garlic and tarragon. Add a good glug of cider
and finish with a spoonful of thick cream. Perfect with steamed beans and creamy mash.*

Pumpkin and ricotta cannelloni Ⓥ 120

*Pumpkin combined with ricotta, Parmesan and lots of fresh herbs, Spoon into cannelloni
and place on a bed of bought tomato pasta sauce. Top with a rich bought cheese sauce,
scatter with Gruyère and bake until golden and bubbling.*

Tuna niçoise platter 123

A platter full of all the elements that make up a niçoise, plus a bit more.

Ribeyes with béarnaise sauce 124

*Perfectly cooked rump steak with a fabulous, easy béarnaise sauce. Serve with a simple
salad and some fries.*

Seafood linguine with coriander pesto

Serves 4 / Ready in 20 minutes

350g linguine

4 tablespoons olive oil

1 bunch spring onions, sliced

3 garlic cloves, chopped

1 red chilli, deseeded and chopped

500g large peeled raw prawns

250g baby plum tomatoes, halved

150g fresh baby spinach

250g fresh white and brown crab meat

juice of 1 lime

for the coriander pesto

25g pine nuts

25g Parmesan, finely grated

1 garlic clove, crushed

8 tablespoons finely chopped coriander

a good squeeze lime juice

6 tablespoons olive oil

This coriander pesto is just gorgeous with prawns or pretty much any type of seafood. It's well worth doubling up on as it'll keep for a good few days in the fridge if you keep the surface of the pesto covered with a slick of olive oil.

To make the pesto by hand, place all of the ingredients in a mortar or small bowl and add a good pinch of coarse salt. Crush with a pestle or the base of a rolling pin to make a thick paste. Check the seasoning and set to one side.

Cook the linguine until *al dente*, drain and set to one side, reserving some of the hot cooking water. Heat a large frying pan or wok until searing hot, add the oil and immediately add the spring onions, garlic and chilli. Stir-fry for 2 minutes, taking care not to let it catch.

Add the prawns and cook over a high heat for 2 minutes. Add the tomatoes and continue to cook until the prawns are cooked through. Season very well.

Tip the pasta back into its hot cooking pot and add the prawn mixture. Add the spinach and crab and a good squeeze of lime. Gently combine, adding some of the reserved hot water if it needs a bit more sauciness. Spoon on to warmed plates and dot with some of the pesto.

Tip

When you cook garlic over such an intense heat, it's very easy for it to catch and give off a bitter flavour. Have an emergency glass of white wine to hand to douse it down if it looks like it might burn. Any excuse . . .

'If you fancy tackling a whole crab yourself, it couldn't be easier to extract the meat. Let the fishmonger do the hard bits for you (easing it open, getting rid of the deadman's fingers, etc.) and then you can just quietly sit and prise out all the delicious meat. One good-sized crab or two smaller ones should yield enough for this recipe.'

Chinese belly pork with wilted spring greens

Serves 4 very generously / Ready in 3 hours, plus refrigeration

1kg piece lean
pork belly

1 teaspoon Maldon
salt, lightly crushed

for the Chinese rub

5 garlic cloves, crushed

2 teaspoons
Chinese five spice

1 tablespoon
brown sugar

1 tablespoon
sunflower oil

1 tablespoon
soy sauce

This dish is unbelievably good. And whilst it's not fancy or overtly glamorous, it does tick all the right boxes if you want something really special without having to spend hours in the kitchen. Once all the prep's done, you just leave it to do its own thing in the oven until achingly tender.

Slash the meat side of the pork all over in a criss-cross fashion and blot with kitchen roll. Lay on a large plate or non-metallic tray, skin-side up. Allow to dry out in the fridge overnight (if you remember) or for a couple of hours if that's all you have.

Preheat the oven to gas 7/220°C/200°C fan.

Combine the rub ingredients and dot all over the meat side of the pork. Rub in really well, making sure that you work it into all of the scored bits.

Tip
There are just a couple of quick tricks when it comes to stir-frying; always heat the wok (or frying pan) up to a really good temperature before adding the oil. Swirl the oil so it coats the pan and then start adding the ingredients. If you do lose that 'sizzle' as you cook, don't be tempted to slosh in more oil. Instead add a tiny splash of water, or wine, or other flavoursome liquid to get things going again.

for the stir-fried greens

1 teaspoon sugar

*3 tablespoons
soy sauce*

*1 tablespoon
sunflower oil*

*1 bunch spring
onions, sliced*

*2 garlic cloves,
finely chopped*

*1 tablespoon finely
chopped fresh ginger*

*500g spring greens,
trimmed and shredded*

to serve

Thai jasmine rice

Line a roasting tin with foil and create a trivet by scrunching up big bits of foil. Lay the pork on top of this, meat-side down. Scatter the salt over the skin and rub in well. Roast for 30 minutes and then reduce the oven temperature to gas 4/180°C/160°C fan. Roast for 2 hours until meltingly tender.

To cook the greens, stir the sugar into the soy, add a splash of water and set to one side. Heat a wok or large frying pan until searing hot, add the oil and swirl. Add the spring onion, garlic and ginger and stir-fry for 2 minutes. Add the greens and almost immediately add the soy mix. Stir-fry for 4 minutes until wilted.

To serve, allow the pork to rest for 5 minutes before cutting into thick chunks. Spoon some hot sticky rice into warmed bowls, top with the greens and some of the pork.

Saturday night special

'I've found that some pieces of pork will produce the most delicious crackling almost by chance whilst others are a little more reluctant. To help things along a little, remove the meat from its packaging and place skin side up on a large plate or platter. Store uncovered overnight in the fridge to allow the skin to dry out. If all else fails, a very careful flash under a hot grill should get things crackling.'

Marmalade-glazed sticky ribs

Serves 4 / Ready in 1 hour, 30 minutes

1kg rack of pork ribs

500ml apple juice

for the marinade

4 tablespoons marmalade

2 tablespoons soy sauce

3 tablespoons sunflower oil

2 garlic cloves, chopped

If there's a barbie on the agenda, I'd move the sossies to one side and put a marmalade-glaze smile on everyone's face instead. Simple, delicious and probably worth making twice the quantity.

Place the ribs in a roasting tin or large pan and pour over the apple juice. Top up with enough water to cover. Bring to the boil, skim off any scum and then simmer for 1 hour until tender. Drain well and pop into a non-metallic bowl.

Combine the marinade ingredients and pour over the ribs. Stir to coat well – use your hands here, it's a lot easier. Allow to marinate for as long as you can. You could do it overnight in the fridge if you're really organized.

When you're ready to eat, cook the ribs over hot coals for 10 minutes, turning and basting as you go until they're sticky and nicely charred. If the barbecue's been rained off, finish them under a hot grill instead for about the same amount of time. Serve with rice, salad and lots of napkins.

Tip

Cooking the ribs in apple juice does several things: it adds lots of flavour, it ensures the meat is as tender as possible and it means you know hand on heart that they're going to be cooked right through when you serve them.

'This delicious glaze is one of my mum's old recipes. She used to add a good sprinkling of Chinese five spice and then slather the whole lot over chicken wings for a really delicious barbie treat.'

Garlicky prawn, clam and chorizo pot

Serves 4 / Ready in 1 hour, 30 minutes

200g chorizo, halved
and thickly sliced

1 large onion, chopped

6 garlic cloves, chopped

1 red pepper,
thickly sliced

1 yellow pepper,
thickly sliced

700g waxy salad
potatoes, peeled
and halved if large

150ml white wine

200g can
chopped tomatoes

250ml hot fish stock

8 large unpeeled
raw prawns

400g large peeled
raw prawns

500g fresh live clams

3 tablespoons chopped
flat-leaf parsley

lemon wedges, to serve

A delicious Spanish-style stew that is just the thing if you've managed to stumble across a good fishmonger whilst out and about.

Heat a large saucepan until hot, add the chorizo and cook for 2–3 minutes until lightly charred and very oily. Remove with a slotted spoon and set to one side. Add the onion to the chorizo oil and cook for 5 minutes. Stir in the garlic and cook for a further 2 minutes, taking care not to burn.

Add the peppers and potatoes. Stir well and then add the wine. Bring to the boil and bubble for a couple of minutes to cook off the alcohol. Add the tomatoes and stock, cover and cook for an hour, stirring every now and then. Add the 8 unpeeled prawns to the pan. After 5 minutes, stir in the chorizo, the peeled prawns and the clams. Cover and cook for 5–10 minutes until the clams have opened and the prawns are pink. Scatter with the parsley and serve with lemon wedges.

Tip

If you can't get hold of clams for this dish, you could simply replace them with the same quantity of live mussels. If you've never dealt with clams before, place them in a bowl of salted water (2 tablespoons in a couple of litres or so should be about right) a couple of hours before you plan to cook them so that they can filter out any grit and sand.

'It's worth hunting out really good-quality yellow-fleshed waxy potatoes for this dish as they add such a delicious flavour, plus they manage to hold a nice firm texture even after the stew has simmered for a long while.'

Vine tomato seared salmon with a lemon and herb dressing

Serves 4 / Ready in 25 minutes

450g cherry vine tomatoes

½ lemon, cut into thick chunks

1 tablespoon olive oil

1 side salmon (around 900g in weight)

for the dressing

2 tablespoons very finely chopped parsley

2 tablespoons very finely chopped chives

2 tablespoons capers, rinsed and chopped

2 tablespoons lemon juice

2 good pinches sugar

5 tablespoons olive oil

1 teaspoon wholegrain mustard

lemon wedges, to serve

To my mind, poached salmon has had its day. This method of roasting a whole side of salmon set on a bed of tomatoes and lemon chunks means optimum flavour and a fantastically moist texture.

Preheat the oven to gas 7/220°C/200°C fan. Place the cherry tomatoes in a roomy roasting tin with their green stalks facing down. Squeeze over the lemon and add the squeezed-out lemon chunks to the tin. Drizzle with half the oil and season well. Lay the salmon over the tomatoes, skin-side up. Drizzle with the remaining oil and season again. Roast for 20 minutes or until cooked through.

Meanwhile, to make the dressing, whisk all the ingredients together and season to taste – remember that you'll get plenty of saltiness from the capers. To serve, take two big fish slices and ask a friend to help turn the salmon out on to a warmed platter. Add lots of lemon wedges and set the dressing on the side. Delicious served with new potatoes and a handful of rocket.

Tip

This dish can also be made in advance and then wheeled out of the fridge later on. If you do decide to try it cold, allow it to sit at room temperature for a little while so that all those flavours can wake up and be counted.

'This is one of my favourite ways of cooking salmon as it's just so simple and ensures a great flavour. If you're cooking for a crowd, this could be just the thing as it's very easy to double up on.'

Aubergine steaks with pesto and griddled flatbreads

Serves 4 / Ready in 45 minutes, plus rising time

2 large aubergines

6 tablespoons olive oil

juice of ½ lemon

75g rocket

25g Parmesan, finely grated

for the pesto

25g pine nuts

25g Parmesan, finely grated

1 garlic clove, crushed

50g fresh basil, chopped

4–6 tablespoons olive oil

for the flatbreads

500g pack white bread mix (e.g. Wright's Premium)

A great barbecue dish for the veggies, although these may have a few meat eaters hot on their tails because of their yum factor . . .

Cut the aubergines lengthways into 4 thick 'steaks'. Score one side in a criss-cross fashion, taking care not to cut all the way through. Drizzle with the oil, squeeze over the lemon and season well. Set to one side.

To make the pesto, place the pine nuts, Parmesan, garlic and a good pinch of salt in a mortar if you have one or a small bowl if you haven't. Crush with the pestle (or a rolling pin) to a thick paste. Work in the basil, adding as much oil as you feel is needed to get a nice thick paste. Season to taste and set to one side.

For the flatbreads, make up the bread mix according to the pack instructions. Allow to rise in the bowl and then tear off a big chunk and roll out to a flat slipper shape. To cook, place the bread on the grill over the hot coals, drizzle with a little oil and turn once it's beginning to puff up and turn golden. This can take anything from 5 to 10 minutes, depending on the heat of the coals.

To cook the aubergine steaks, spread some of the pesto over the cut side and work it into the scored flesh a little. Place on the barbie, cut-side up, and cook for 5 minutes or so until beginning to soften. Flip and cook for a further 5 minutes and keep going until the aubergine is soft and unctuous. To serve, place a slice or two of aubergine on each plate, scatter with some rocket and extra Parmesan, add an extra spoonful of pesto and pop some bread on the side.

Tip
If cooking the flatbreads on the barbie seems like a step too far, then simply plump for pittas or shop-bought flatbreads and warm through on the barbie instead.

'I adore aubergine, but it does have to be cooked really well – and that means you need to pile on the flavour and seasonings, use plenty of oil and keep on cooking until it is soft and velvety. There's nothing worse than undercooked squeaky aubergine.'

Chicken in cider, garlic and tarragon sauce

Serves 4 / Ready in 40 minutes

2 tablespoons olive oil

4 part-boned chicken breasts

25g butter

4 shallots, finely chopped

4 garlic cloves, finely chopped

200ml medium sweet cider

200ml chicken stock

200ml double cream

4 tablespoons chopped tarragon

This dish is simplicity itself, but it's guaranteed to have everyone raving.

Heat the oil in a large non-stick frying pan. Add the chicken, skin-side down, and cook over a medium-high heat until golden all over. Remove from the pan and set to one side for a moment.

Add the butter to the pan and heat until gently foaming. Add the shallots and garlic and cook for 5 minutes until perfectly softened. Add the cider, bring to the boil and scrape up any yummy bits from the base of the pan with a wooden spoon.

Return the chicken to the pan, add the stock and bring to the boil. Cover and simmer for 15 minutes until cooked through. Place the chicken on a warm serving platter.

Add the cream to the pan and bubble rapidly until thickened. Stir in the tarragon and check the seasoning. Pour over the chicken and serve with steamed green beans.

Tip

I always tend to go for part-boned chicken breasts as they seem to have more flavour and stay moister. Look out for them in supermarkets or ask your butcher for them in advance if it's not his usual thing.

'If you're not planning on anything too OTT for your pudding, I'd be tempted to serve this chicken with buttery mash to soak up all that lovely sauce.'

Pumpkin and ricotta cannelloni

Serves 4 / Ready in 1 hour, 10 minutes

350g jar good-quality
tomato pasta sauce

12 cannelloni tubes

350g pot good-quality
fresh cheese sauce

3 tablespoons milk

50g Gruyère cheese,
finely grated

for the filling

1 tablespoon olive oil

600g pumpkin or
squash, peeled and diced

2 fat garlic cloves,
chopped

100ml white wine

150g ricotta cheese

50g Parmesan
cheese, finely grated

4 tablespoons
chopped basil

I love this dish – I think it's the combination of the sweet pumpkin with all the cheeses that gives it that wonderful flavour. And if you're quick enough to hide the evidence, no one will ever know you used bought sauces!

To make the filling, heat the oil in a large frying pan, add the pumpkin and cook over a medium heat for 15 minutes until softened. Add the garlic and cook for 2–3 minutes. Add the wine, bubble rapidly to cook off and then remove from the heat.

Preheat the oven to gas 5/190°C/170°C fan. Place the pumpkin mixture in a bowl and add the ricotta, Parmesan and basil. Combine well and try a little bit at this stage to see just how much seasoning it needs.

Pour the tomato sauce into the base of a large baking dish and fill the cannelloni tubes with the pumpkin mixture. Lay them on top of the sauce. Spoon the cheese sauce into a jug and add the milk. Pour this over the cannelloni and then finish with the Gruyère. Bake for 35 minutes or until tender, bubbling and golden on top.

Tip

The pumpkin filling could quite easily be made a day or two before and stored in the fridge ready for assembly. If you really wanted to get ahead, you could make the whole thing in advance and freeze uncooked in its dish ready to be wheeled to its destination.

'I used to be really put off cooking cannelloni dishes as I loathed all that fiddling and stuffing the tubes – it's the same annoyed feeling I get when trying to stuff a duvet into a cover the wrong way round! But I'm now a convert ... With a bit of practice and a small enough spoon, it's really not that tricky. And if you really do hate it, ask someone else to do it for you!'

Tuna niçoise platter

Serves 4 / Ready in 25 minutes

500g new potatoes,
halved

6 eggs

200g fine beans, trimmed

1 head cos lettuce,
leaves separated

250g mixed tomatoes,
cut into bite-sized chunks

175g chargrilled
artichokes, drained

75g fresh anchovies,
drained

100g mixed olives, drained

500g fresh tuna steaks

1 tablespoon olive oil

for the dressing

1 tablespoon
red wine vinegar

3 tablespoons chopped
fresh parsley

2 tablespoons capers,
rinsed and chopped

4 tablespoons
extra virgin olive oil

1 teaspoon sugar

I love serving this platter when I've got a big group of friends coming over. That way, everyone can just help themselves to whatever part of the salad takes their fancy.

Cook the potatoes until tender, drain and set to one side. Boil the eggs in water until just set. Steam the beans until tender, refresh under cold water and set to one side. Combine the dressing ingredients, season to taste and set to one side. Arrange the salad ingredients on a large platter and set to one side.

Preheat a non-stick frying pan until searing hot and drizzle the tuna with the oil. Season well and cook over a high heat for 2 minutes on each side or until done as you like it. Roughly break up and add to the salad. Serve straight away with the dressing on the side. Delicious served with plenty of fresh French bread.

Tip
Always cook the tuna just before you're ready to serve, but the rest can be prepared an hour or so in advance. If it's a particularly hot day, store in the fridge but do allow to stand at room temperature for 30 minutes or so before serving.

'I've been making this dish in many guises over the years – sometimes adding antipasto peppers, sometimes quails' eggs and I once tried it with salmon. The varieties are endless . . .'

Ribeyes with béarnaise sauce

Serves 4 / Ready in 20 minutes

4 × 250g ribeye steaks

1 tablespoon sunflower oil

for the sauce

3 tablespoons white wine vinegar

1 shallot, finely chopped

2 tablespoons chopped tarragon

2 egg yolks

150g butter, melted

Ribeyes are my desert-island steak! Deep red, marbled with fat and absolutely packed with flavour: to my mind, there's nothing like them.

Place the vinegar, shallots and tarragon in a small saucepan with 2 tablespoons water. Bring to the boil and bubble until there is barely a tablespoon of liquid left. Pour into a large heatproof bowl and allow to cool a little.

Add the egg yolks and place the bowl over a pan of very, very gently simmering water. Whisk like mad until the whisk leaves a trail in the mixture as it slightly thickens. Remove from the pan and start adding the butter a little at a time, vigorously whisking all the while. Season well and keep warm until the steaks are ready.

To cook the steaks, drizzle them with the oil and season well. Preheat (preferably two!) large frying pans until blistering hot. Add the steaks and cook for 2–3 minutes before turning and cooking for another 2–3 minutes. Allow to stand before serving with the sauce. Delicious with a lovely big salad and hot chips.

Tip

Don't let your béarnaise sit around for too long – really you should start thinking about putting the steaks on once you begin adding the butter to the egg mixture. Once done, I tend to let it sit on the pan (turned off) with the hot water in, just so it doesn't cool too quickly.

'I know I've been raving about my favourite cut of meat when it comes to steak, but before I get too full of myself (or before anyone else around you does), always remember this great quote from John Torode's fantastic book, Beef: "Cooking steak is a joy because it is a terrific piece of meat with flavour whether grilled or fried, and there are no rules. Apart from this: eat the steak cooked the way you like it and tell the steak snobs to rack off – we all have personal taste." What a man!'

Sunday lunch

If you want to win hearts and friends and maybe secure an afternoon with your feet up in the process, cook up a big, fat, lovely Sunday lunch for everyone.

I don't know why I love Sunday lunches so much. Maybe it's because for us Sunday was traditionally the day we all stayed together as a family without the distraction of shops and boring weekly chores and we all sat down together and ate during the day. I love spending Sundays with friends and my own young family, as everyone really does seem to muck in and have fun peeling veg, chopping tatties, topping up wine glasses and stirring the gravy.

If the day's plans include a walk, followed by a pint in a pub, go for a slow-cooked number that will happily sit on the stove for an hour or so and then maybe need just a little bit of attention on your return. The beef and Black Sheep ale pie is the perfect contender as it gets better and better the longer it cooks. All you then need to do is pop on a pastry lid and steam some veggies for a fantastic lunch that warms the soul. Another great option would be the sausage cassoulet as it will cook to perfection over several hours, leaving you free to wind down and enjoy the day.

But no matter what, I couldn't imagine Sunday lunch without a couple of Yorkshires on the side – and for me it doesn't matter if they're to accompany roast beef, lamb or pork. I just love them and so do my children. If you fancy making some and don't have any scales to hand, don't worry – my yogurt-pot Yorkshires recipe uses yogurt pots as a measure for the flour, resulting in fantastic Yorkshires every time.

Easy eats for a relaxing Sunday

Beef and Black Sheep ale pie 130

A slow-cooked beef stew flavoured with Black Sheep ale, shallots and thyme. Top with a ready-rolled sheet of puff pastry. No need to trim: just glaze and bake until golden and risen.

Moroccan leg of lamb with chickpeas 133

Score a leg of lamb and rub with a paste of dried apricots, preserved lemons and garlic. Roast on a bed of chickpeas, stock and tomatoes flavoured with rose harissa. Serve with buttered couscous.

Fennel and pear roast pork 134

Shoulder of pork slow-roasted with thick wedges of fennel and halved pears. Flavour with a glug of white wine and plenty of thyme. Lovely with mash and steamed veggies.

Slow-cooked chorizo and garlic roast chicken 137

Two chickens roasted with chopped chorizo, garlic, wine and rosemary. Start them off upside-down to keep them as tender and juicy as possible. Turn and then cook until golden. Serve with mash and all the yummy pan juices.

Sausage cassoulet 138

A rich slow-cooked cassoulet with thick sausages and haricot beans cooked in wine, stock and herbs. Serve with thick slices of garlic bread.

Chicken pot pies 141

Chunks of ready-roasted chicken stirred into a creamy wine and leek sauce. Spoon into ramekins or small tins and top with rounds of ready-rolled shortcrust pastry. Bake until golden and serve with steamed veg.

Mushroom-stuffed pork fillet 142

Two whole fillets of pork opened out and filled with a mushroom, herb and sausagemeat stuffing. Sandwich, tie together and roast with a glug of Marsala and some garlic cloves. Serve with veg and chilled Marsala.

Shallot and chestnut stew ⓥ 147

A chunky veggie stew with shallots, mushrooms and whole chestnuts in a rich red wine and redcurrant gravy. Delicious spooned into a giant Yorkshire with a splodge of English mustard.

Yogurt-pot Yorkshires 148

Perfect Yorkshire puddings made by measuring the ingredients in a yogurt pot – no need for scales.

Horseradish- and sugar-crusted beef 151

A stonking great piece of beef basted with brown sugar and hot horseradish, roasted until perfectly pink and served with roasties, Yorkshires and plenty of gravy.

Beef and Black Sheep ale pie

Serves 4 very generously / Ready in 3 hours

150g smoked streaky bacon, chopped

300g banana shallots, halved

3 carrots, thickly sliced

3 celery sticks, thickly sliced

300g chestnut mushrooms

2 garlic cloves, chopped

800g braising steak, cut into large chunks

50g plain flour

1–2 tablespoons sunflower oil

500ml Black Sheep ale

400ml beef stock

2 tablespoons chopped thyme

2 bay leaves

1 egg, beaten

375g pack ready-made, ready-rolled puff pastry

Rich, comforting and in actual fact a pretty economical way of cooking a very satisfying Sunday lunch for a big group of friends.

Heat a large ovenproof casserole dish, add the bacon and fry for 5 minutes until golden. Remove with a slotted spoon and set aside. Add the shallots, carrots, celery, mushrooms and garlic and cook for a further 5 minutes. Remove from the pan with a slotted spoon and add to the bacon.

Dredge the beef with the flour and season well. Heat the oil in the pan and fry the beef in batches until well browned all over. Return the veggies and bacon to the beef and add the ale, stock and herbs. Bring to the boil, stirring constantly, until bubbling.

Reduce the heat and cover. Simmer for 1 hour, 30 minutes, stirring every now and then. Meanwhile, preheat the oven to gas 7/220°C/200°C fan. Remove the lid and cook the stew for a further 30 minutes until thickened and rich.

Wet the rim of the casserole dish with the beaten egg and lay the sheet of pastry over the top. Trim a little off if you like and then brush with the remainder of the egg. Cut a few vents in the pastry and bake for 20–25 minutes until golden and risen.

Make & take ...

Wonderfully rich stews like this always taste better if you make them a day or two before, so why not take one you made earlier and then simply heat through, top with pastry and bake? The stew also freezes really well.

'The beauty of this dish is that you need do very little rolling and messing around with pastry. Simply pop on top, trim a little if there's a huge overhang and then bake until crisp and golden.'

Moroccan leg of lamb with chickpeas

Serves 4 very, very generously / Ready in 2 hours, 20 minutes

2kg lamb leg

for the marinade

2 garlic cloves,
very finely chopped

100g ready-to-eat dried
apricots, finely chopped

2 preserved lemons,
finely chopped

1 tablespoon olive oil

for the chickpeas

2 tablespoons olive oil

2 red onions, sliced

6 garlic cloves, chopped

1 tablespoon chopped ginger

2 tablespoons rose harissa
paste (e.g. Belazu)

2 x 400g cans chickpeas,
drained and rinsed

1 cinnamon stick

250ml chicken stock

500g cherry vine tomatoes

6 tablespoons chopped
fresh coriander

A fantastically simple, flavour-packed dish that's perfect if you fancy something just that little bit different.

Preheat the oven to gas 5/190°C/170°C fan. Set the lamb on a chopping board and slash the flesh all over, about 2cm deep in a criss-cross pattern. Combine the marinade ingredients and rub all over the lamb, working it into the meat.

Heat the oil in a large roasting tin that will sit on a hob. Add the onion and garlic and cook for 5 minutes. Add the ginger and harissa and cook for a couple of minutes more until fragrant. Add the chickpeas, cinnamon and chicken stock and bring to the boil. Turn off the heat.

Set the lamb on top of the chickpeas and roast in the oven for 30 minutes per 450g, basting every now and then and stirring the chickpeas as it cooks. 30 minutes before the end of cooking time, lay the tomatoes on top of the chickpeas and return to the oven.

Allow the lamb to rest for 15 minutes before carving. Stir the coriander into the chickpeas and serve with thick slices of lamb and some hot buttery couscous.

Tip

Keep an eye on the lamb for the last 30 minutes or so of cooking as the sugary apricots can burn if there are any hotspots. If it begins to look a little dark, cover loosely with foil.

'There are a few ready-made jars of harissa on the market now and they all seem to have varying degrees of heat about them. Be guided by the pack instructions but also give them a little taste before you start spooning them in and trust your taste buds.'

Fennel and pear roast pork

Serves 6–8 / Ready in 3 hours, 50 minutes, plus resting

2½kg shoulder of
pork, skin scored

1 tablespoon oil

1 teaspoon salt

2 large heads
fennel, trimmed

4 ripe Conference
pears

200ml white wine

a few sprigs of thyme

for the gravy

2 tablespoons
sunflower oil

2 tablespoons
plain flour

The tender roasted pears and fennel taste just gorgeous with the rich pork. Lovely with buttery mash and steamed greens.

Preheat the oven to gas 7/220°C/200°C fan. Drizzle the pork with the oil, scatter with the salt and rub into the scored skin. Place the pork directly on the oven shelf in the middle of the oven with the tin underneath. Roast for 30 minutes, then reduce the heat to gas 5/190°C/170°C fan. Roast for a further 35 minutes per 450g.

Cut the fennel into wedges and the pears into thick wedges, removing the core. Place in the roasting tin that has been sat underneath the pork and add the wine, thyme sprigs and plenty of seasoning. Once the pork has been cooking at the lower temperature for 1 hour, put the vegetables in the oven, back under the pork, for a further 1 hour, 30 minutes until tender.

Whilst you allow the pork to rest for 30 minutes, spoon off any fat from the vegetables and then drain them, reserving the goodness in a jug. Make the volume up to 450ml with water or light stock.

To make the gravy, heat the oil in a saucepan, add the flour and cook for a couple of minutes before whisking in the goodness and stock. Bring to the boil and then simmer for 10 minutes or until thickened to how you like it. Carve the pork and serve with the roasted fennel and apple and a good slick of gravy.

Tip
Your joint of pork will generally come already scored, but ask your butcher to add lots more if you can as it will help to produce even better crackling.

'I'd always go for shoulder of pork rather than leg as it's much more tender and way more juicy, probably due to the layers of fat within it.'

Slow-cooked chorizo and garlic roast chicken

Serves 8 / Ready in 2 hours, 15 minutes

260g pack chorizo sausage, cut into thick slices

3 bulbs garlic, halved

100ml white wine

2 red peppers, cut into thick chunks

2 heads fennel, cut into wedges

2 big sprigs fresh rosemary

3 tablespoons olive oil

2 whole free-range chickens

I love roast chicken but there never seems to be enough if you're cooking for any kind of a crowd. Roasting two looks lovely and the slightly longer cooking time means heaps more flavour.

Preheat the oven to gas 5/190°C/170°C fan. Place the chorizo in a large roasting tin along with the garlic, wine, peppers, fennel and rosemary and drizzle with half the oil.

Place the chickens on top of the veg and drizzle with the remaining oil. Season everything well and place in the oven. Cook for 2 hours, basting the chickens every now and then until golden and cooked through.

Tip

I always roast my chooks upside-down for the first hour of cooking. This way, the white breast meat stays fantastically moist and absorbs all the flavours from the roasting tin. Turn the right way round for the last bit of roasting to crisp and colour the skin.

'All those delicious juices in the bottom of the roasting tin make a gorgeous instant gravy. Pour into a jug, skim off any fat and then keep warm with all the roasted veg and garlic. Delicious spooned over mash.'

Sausage cassoulet

Serves 4 / Ready in 4 hours, plus overnight soaking

300g haricot beans, soaked overnight

1 tablespoon olive oil

8 thick sausages

150g lardons

1 large onion, chopped

4 celery stalks, thickly sliced

4 garlic cloves, chopped

750ml hot chicken stock

300ml white wine

2 tablespoons tomato purée

2 tablespoons chopped thyme

2 bay leaves

This dish is one of my recent addictions! I love the fact that it will very happily sit in the oven for an extra half-hour or so if you're not quite ready and I love the warming effect it has on the whole kitchen – perfect after a long wintery walk.

Drain the soaked beans and place in a pan with plenty of fresh water. Bring to the boil and then boil for 10 minutes, spooning off any foam from the surface. Reduce the heat and simmer for 1 hour. Drain and set to one side.

Preheat the oven to gas 3/170°C/150°C fan. Heat the oil in a large flameproof casserole, add the sausages and brown all over for about 10 minutes. Remove from the pan, set aside and then add the lardons. Cook for 5 minutes until well browned. Remove from the pan with a slotted spoon and set aside with the sausages.

Add the onion and celery to the pan and cook for 10 minutes until softened. Add the garlic and cook for a further 2 minutes. Add the beans and stir in the sausages and lardons. Pour over the stock and wine and stir in the tomato purée, thyme and bay leaf.

Cover and cook for 2 hours. Remove the lid and cook for a further hour, stirring every now and then. Spoon into warmed bowls and serve with plenty of fresh bread to get every last bit of sauce.

Tip

Make sure you use a very light stock with not too much salt for this one, as both the sausages and the lardons have more than enough to season the dish.

'If washing-up really isn't your thing or you have no willing helpers to hand, then this should be your first choice for a perfectly relaxed Sunday afternoon.'

Chicken pot pies

Serves 4 / Ready in 1 hour

50g butter

1 large leek, sliced

150g mushrooms, roughly chopped

3 garlic cloves, chopped

2 tablespoons chopped thyme

40g plain flour

150ml white wine

500ml chicken stock

400g roast chicken, cut into bite-sized pieces

100ml crème fraîche

4 tablespoons chopped parsley

250g ready-made, ready-rolled puff pastry

1 egg, beaten

My kids absolutely adore these cute little pies. Use lots of small mismatched pots for cooking them in and go as OTT as you fancy decorating the top.

Heat the butter in a large non-stick frying pan, add the leek and cook for 5 minutes until softened. Add the mushrooms, garlic and thyme and cook for a further 5 minutes. Stir in the flour and cook for 3 minutes, continuing to stir. Add the wine and stock, bring to boil and then simmer for a couple of minutes.

Preheat the oven to gas 6/200°C/180°C fan. Add the chicken and crème fraîche to the pan, check the seasoning and heat through for a couple of minutes. Stir in the parsley. Spoon the filling into 4 × 250ml ovenproof dishes and set aside.

Cut out the pastry to fit the top of the pie dishes. Brush the pie rims with egg and then place a pastry lid on each. Cut a vent in each pie and brush with egg. Place the pies on a big roasting tin and bake for 15–20 minutes until golden and bubbling.

Tip

You can either buy ready-roast chicken from the supermarket or roast your own. One medium-sized chicken will give you around 500g cooked meat.

'If you like, you could always cook this as one big pie – just spoon the filling into a roomy ovenproof dish and top with the pastry. Cut a vent for the steam, glaze and bake as normal.'

Mushroom-stuffed pork fillet

Serves 4–6 / Ready in 1 hour, 30 minutes

15g porcini mushrooms

25g butter

150g chestnut mushrooms, chopped

1 tablespoon chopped sage, plus extra leaves for tying

450g good-quality sausagemeat

2 x 400g pork fillets

1 tablespoon oil

150ml Marsala

150ml chicken stock

6 garlic cloves

3 tablespoons double cream

A really simple, fail-safe roast that requires little more than a few crisp roasties and some steamed veg.

Preheat the oven to gas 5/190°C/170°C fan. Place the porcini mushrooms in a bowl and cover with boiling water. Set aside for 15 minutes to rehydrate. Drain and squeeze out any excess water.

Melt the butter in a large non-stick frying pan, add the chestnut mushrooms and cook for 5 minutes. Add the porcini mushrooms and cook for 2 minutes until all the moisture has been driven off. Remove from the heat and allow to cool a little before mixing with the sage and sausagemeat.

Place one of the fillets on a chopping board and make a cut right along its length without cutting all the way through. Make another cut right along its length a couple of centimetres away from your first cut and do the same to the other side of the first cut. This will help 'open out' the fillet, making it wider. Repeat with the other fillet.

Place the stuffing along one of the fillets and top with the other one. Secure in place with string all along the length. Push some extra sage leaves under the string and then drizzle with the oil and season. Heat a large non-stick frying pan and add the pork. Cook over a high heat until brown all over. Place in a roasting tin and set to one side.

Pour the Marsala into the frying pan and heat and stir to scrape up any yummy bits – watch out as it may flame. Add the stock and then pour over the pork. Scatter with the garlic cloves and cook for 1 hour, basting every now and then if you remember, until cooked through. Allow to stand before carving.

To make the sauce, place the roasting tin with all its cooking juices on the hob and bubble for 2 minutes. Stir in the cream, bubble briefly and then pour into a warmed jug to serve alongside the pork.

Tip
Don't go for a huge roasting tin for this one – if it's too big, all the lovely Marsala and stock will cook off completely, leaving you with nothing for the base of your sauce.

'It doesn't matter how haphazard the fillets look when stuffed and tied together. Once roasted and thickly sliced, they're a dream.'

Shallot and chestnut stew

Serves 4 / Ready in 45 minutes

1 tablespoon oil

250g large
shallots, halved

2 carrots,
thickly sliced

250g white
mushrooms,
halved or quartered

2 garlic cloves,
chopped

1 tablespoon
chopped thyme

2 tablespoons
plain flour

200ml red wine

300ml light
vegetable stock

200g vacuum-
packed chestnuts,
roughly chopped

150g kale,
roughly chopped

1–2 tablespoons
redcurrant jelly

Each and every vegetarian will fall instantly in love with you when you wheel this out of the kitchen served in lovely big crisp Yorkshire puddings.

Preheat the oil in a large saucepan, add the shallots and carrots and cook for 10 minutes until lightly caramelized. Add the mushrooms, garlic and thyme and cook for 5 minutes.

Stir in the flour and cook whilst stirring for 3 minutes. Add the red wine to the pan and whisk like mad, scraping up any flour or crusty bits from the base of the pan. Bubble for 2 minutes to cook off the alcohol.

Add the stock and chestnuts, and simmer for a couple of minutes before adding the kale. Simmer for just under 10 minutes or until the kale and carrots are tender. Stir in the redcurrant jelly (taste as you whisk it in) and season to taste.

Tip

If your gravy isn't quite as thick as you'd like, simply whisk in a teaspoon or so of vegetarian gravy granules and bubble until thick.

'A rich, satisfying veggie stew capable of wooing any meat eater to the table.'

Yogurt-pot Yorkshires

Makes 12 small puddings or 4 larger ones / Ready in 20 minutes

3 tablespoons oil

2 yogurt-pot measures
of plain flour

2 eggs

200ml milk

I have the lovely Ceiridwen to thank for this very clever idea – perfectly crisp, light Yorkshires without the need for scales ...

Preheat the oven to gas 6/200°C/180°C fan. Drizzle the oil into the holes of the Yorkshire pudding tin and heat in the oven until smoking.

Place the flour in a large bowl, add a good pinch of salt and then add the eggs and milk. Beat until smooth. Pour the batter into the hot fat and bake for 15 minutes until golden and risen.

Tip
Two individual yogurt pots filled (not packed) with plain flour is equivalent to 125g or 225ml of flour tipped into a measuring jug.

'Making Yorkshire puddings isn't rocket science – you don't need to be fantastically accurate with your measurements, but you definitely need two eggs, a batter the consistency of double cream and smoking-hot oil at the ready in the tins.'

Horseradish- and sugar-crusted beef

Serves 4 / Ready in 1 hour, 40 minutes, plus resting

3 tablespoons grated hot horseradish from a jar

2 tablespoons soft brown sugar

1kg piece of topside

Simple beyond belief, but the combination of fiery horseradish and sweet soft brown sugar is a hit.

Preheat the oven to gas 7/220°C/200°C fan. Combine the horseradish and sugar in a bowl and then slather all over the beef. Season with pepper and then roast for 20 minutes.

Reduce the oven to gas 5/190°C/170°C fan and then roast for 25 minutes per 450g plus 25 minutes. Allow to stand for 20 minutes or so before carving.

Tip
Always let joints of meat sit at room temperature for an hour or so before roasting – that way, they won't be really chilly in the centre as they hit the heat of the oven.

'If you can, cook the meat directly on the oven shelf with a roasting tin positioned underneath to catch any of the juices. It gives a fantastic all-round colour and flavour to the joint.'

Puddings

Sadly, puddings are one of the first things that are forgotten about in the effort to pack more into the day and it's such a shame. I'm not for one minute suggesting that every meal should be punctuated with a big, hefty pudding or some tricky dessert, but if the time is right and you fancy a treat, why not?

The trick is to choose your pudding according to the time you have available and the amount of energy you actually want to expend. If time is tight, go for clever little puds that need little more than a quick assembly job on the day. My cheat's trifle is just that – a list of simple, great-quality ingredients that just need to be layered-up an hour or so ahead of time.

I can't think of a simpler, more decadent way to end a lovely dinner with the grown-ups than with a little shot glass filled with a very simple bourbon-laced chocolate ganache. Serve straight from the fridge, *à la* 'Here's one I made earlier!' and accompany with an icy-cold shot of bourbon – it's a kind of sip, spoon, sip, sip treat that's the perfect way to end a great night in.

Something sweet to end your dinner in style

Pear and vanilla tarte Tatin 159

A simple, delicious pudding, the perfect end to an autumnal lunch. Caramelized pear and vanilla topped with ready-made shortcrust and baked.

Chocolate bourbon pots 160

An indulgent pud that needs only three ingredients: bitter chocolate, bourbon and cream. Serve with iced bourbon shots.

Any-fruit streusel cake 163

A delicious 'bake and take' cake that can be made with just about any fruit you fancy. Rich, moist sponge topped with roasted rhubarb, blueberry and raspberry, or ripe plums. Scatter with the streusel topping and bake.

Nectarine tart 164

No tin, no measuring and just three ingredients make up this stunning tart. Just scatter ready-rolled puff pastry with halved nectarines and a little sugar, then bake. Substitute chunks of apricot if you prefer.

Chocolate beetroot cake 167

Another great bake-ahead cake that becomes moister after a day or so of storing. Rich, chocolaty and dense. Top with a rich dark chocolate frosting.

Tropical-fruit Eton mess 168

Mango and papaya stirred through whipped cream and crushed meringue. The perfect instant pud.

Steamed jug pudding 171

A really lovely traditional syrup pudding that doesn't need scales. Simply measure the ingredients in a jug, pour into the pudding basin and steam for a couple of hours. Lovely with lots of hot custard.

Champagne and raspberry jellies 172

Jelly cubes melted with hot water and topped up with Cava and Chambord. Drop fresh raspberries into wine glasses or Champagne flutes, pour over the cooled jelly and allow to set.

Chocolate-muffin and raspberry trifle 175

A bit of an assembly job! Scatter sliced chocolate muffins in the base of a trifle dish. Drizzle with Crème de cassis or Chambord, scatter with fresh raspberries and top with ready-made custard and lightly whipped cream. Go as OTT as you fancy with chocolate curls and raspberries for the top.

Plum crumble 176

Scatter a simple, light crumble topping over plums (or any seasonal fruits) and bake. Serve hot with custard or cream.

Pear and vanilla tarte Tatin

Serves 6 / Ready in 45 minutes

75g butter, chopped

75g caster sugar

6 Williams pears, peeled and cored

1 vanilla pod, split

350g ready-made, ready-rolled shortcrust pastry

A very simple but truly stunning pudding that needs nothing more than a scoop of ice-cream or a spoonful of cool crème fraîche.

Preheat the oven to gas 6/200°C/180°C fan. Dot the butter over the base of a 25cm ovenproof frying pan and sprinkle the sugar over the top. Cut the pears into thick wedges and arrange on top of the sugar, nudging the vanilla pod in between.

Gently heat the butter and sugar over a low heat. After about 10 minutes the butter and the sugar should be nicely liquid. Turn up the heat a little and cook for 15 minutes until lovely and caramelized – shake the pan every now and then. Remove from the heat.

Cut a 25cm circle out of the pastry and carefully place on top of the pears. Tuck the edges down the side of the pears to encase them completely. Bake in the oven for 20 minutes until golden. Very carefully turn out on to a serving plate and serve hot with ice-cream or crème fraîche.

Tip

If you fancy a more traditional Tatin, try using crisp eating apples instead of pears. Around 8 peeled and cored Cox's should do it.

'If you want to make a truly fabulous tarte Tatin, there's no getting away from it – you've got to be brave and cook the buttery mixture until it is really well caramelized. And don't take your eyes off it as it can burn in the blink of an eye!'

Chocolate bourbon pots

Serves 4 / Ready in 10 minutes, plus chilling

150g dark chocolate,
broken up

142ml pot
double cream

2–3 tablespoons
bourbon whiskey

dark chocolate
curls, to serve

A fantastically rich dessert that can be made a day in advance if you like.

Melt the chocolate in a heatproof bowl set over a pan of very gently simmering water. Add the cream and Bourbon and whisk until smooth and glossy. Pour into four shot glasses. Allow to cool before chilling for an hour or until needed.

Tip

Combine the chocolate, cream and bourbon in a jug as it makes it so much easier to pour into the little glasses.

'If bourbon isn't your thing, try Cognac or Cointreau. Or if you want to keep it completely teetotal, a good shot of espresso will pack a punch.'

Any-fruit streusel cake

Serves 8 / Ready in 1 hour

for the
streusel topping

75g plain flour

50g unsalted butter

50g demerara sugar

50g flaked almonds

for the cake

225g self-raising flour

*1 teaspoon
baking powder*

*125g unsalted butter,
cubed, plus extra
for greasing*

*100g golden
caster sugar*

2 eggs, beaten

3 tablespoons milk

for the topping

*300g mixed ripe fruit
(see below)*

*The perfect bake-and-take cake for any weekend away –
and the great thing is, it tastes even better a day or so
after making.*

Preheat the oven to gas 4/170°C/150°C fan. Butter
a 23cm springform cake tin and line the base with
greaseproof paper. To make the streusel topping, place
the flour and butter in a bowl and rub together until the
mixture resembles lumpy breadcrumbs. Stir in the sugar
and almonds.

To make the cake mix, place the flour, baking powder
and butter in a large bowl and rub until the mixture
resembles breadcrumbs. Stir in the sugar and then
mix in the eggs and enough milk to give a dropping
consistency.

Spoon into the prepared tin, level off the top and
scatter with your chosen fruit. Scatter the streusel mixture
over and then bake for 35–40 minutes. Test with a skewer
to ensure the cake is cooked through. Allow to sit in the
tin for 15 minutes before cooling on a rack.

Tip

You can use just about any fruit you fancy on this cake. Ripe pears, plums or
apples would be great, or go for blueberries, peaches or raspberries. The options
are endless.

*'This recipe is an old favourite of mine. If I ever need to do a production line of
cakes for parties or school fêtes, this is the one I go for. It travels well, gets better
with age and it always looks the business.'*

Nectarine tart

Serves 8 / Ready in 20 minutes

*500g ready-made,
ready-rolled
puff pastry*

*8 nectarines, halved
and stoned*

25g caster sugar

*No scales, no measuring and no tricky techniques are
needed to make this stunning tart. All you need are
three ingredients and one hot oven!*

Preheat the oven to gas 7/220°C/200°C fan. Place the
pastry on a work surface and roll out further to fit
the dimensions of your largest flat baking sheet.
    Place on the baking sheet and score a 2cm rim all
the way round the pastry. Scatter over the nectarines
and sugar and bake for 15 minutes until golden and
risen. Slice and serve warm with cream or ice-cream.

Tip
Ready-rolled pastry needs to sit at room temperature for 30 minutes or so before
you attempt to unroll it as it can fracture if it's still too hard from the fridge.

*'Try this tart served with softly whipped double cream pepped up with a tiny bit
of vanilla extract and a spoonful or so of sifted icing sugar – sublime!'*

Chocolate beetroot cake

Serves 8 / Ready in 1 hour

2 large eggs

150g soft brown sugar

75ml sunflower oil

150g dark chocolate,
melted and cooled

1 teaspoon
vanilla extract

75g self-raising
flour, sifted

½ teaspoon
baking powder

40g ground almonds

150g raw beetroot,
peeled and grated

for the icing

100g dark chocolate,
broken into pieces

25g butter, plus
extra for greasing
the cake tin

3 tablespoons
double cream

50g icing sugar, sifted

Intensely rich and chocolatey, the beetroot gives it a fantastic dense moist texture that means it will happily keep for several days.

Preheat the oven to gas 4/180°C/160°C fan. Butter a 2lb loaf tin and line the base with greaseproof paper. Place the eggs, sugar and oil in a large mixing bowl and beat together with an electric whisk for about 3 minutes until foaming.

Stir in the chocolate and vanilla extract and then carefully fold in the flour, baking powder and ground almonds. Fold in the beetroot, and then spoon into the prepared tin. Bake for 45 minutes until set. Test the cake by inserting a wooden skewer and give it an extra 5 minutes if needed. Allow to cool in the tin for 10 minutes before transferring to a rack to cool completely.

To make the icing, melt the chocolate and butter in a bowl over a pan of simmering water. Remove from the heat, cool a little and beat in the cream and icing sugar. Allow to cool and harden a little before roughly spreading over the top of the cake.

Tip

If you're travelling with this cake, run a long, wide strip of greaseproof paper along the length of the tin with plenty of overhang at each end. Return the cooled, iced cake to the tin and loosely wrap with greaseproof and cling film. The overhanging paper will help you lift it out easily once you're ready to eat.

'I prefer to coarsely grate the beetroot when I make this cake as it gives it a really lovely texture with discernible flecks of beetroot. If you fancy a finer texture, just grate the beetroot more finely.'

Tropical-fruit Eton mess

Serves 4 / Ready in 10 minutes

200ml double cream, lightly whipped

150g pot 0% fat Greek yogurt

1 large ripe mango, stoned, peeled and diced

1 papaya, deseeded, peeled and diced

50g meringues, roughly crushed

2 passion fruit, halved

When red berries are out of season and astronomically expensive, this tropical version of the classic is a fantastic alternative.

Combine the cream, yogurt, mango, papaya and meringues. Stir in all but one half of the passion-fruit pulp and then spoon into glasses. Top with the remaining passion-fruit pulp and serve.

Tip
If you want to get ahead with this one, make it up bar the meringues, as they'll go a bit too mushy if they sit around for any length of time.

'Using a combination of cream and fat-free yogurt results in a pud that's not quite so scarily laden with calories, plus it really lifts the flavour.'

Steamed jug pudding

Serves 6 / Ready in 1 hour, 45 minutes

6 tablespoons
golden syrup

200g butter, softened,
plus extra for greasing

200ml golden caster
sugar (200g)

1 vanilla pod,
split open

4 eggs, beaten

300ml self-raising
flour, sifted (200g)

3–4 tablespoons milk

I can't tell you how much I love this pudding – it's so, so simple to make but the long cooking time gives it the most sublime texture and flavour. If you do fancy making this whilst you're away and haven't any scales for measuring, I've included ml measures for a measuring jug (hence the name!) Be sure not to pack the sugar or flour down when you measure it out: just spoon in and level off.

Butter a 1 litre pudding basin and place a circle of greaseproof paper in the base. Drizzle the syrup into the bottom and set to one side. Cut out a square of foil and a square of greaseproof paper that are large enough to go over the pudding with plenty of room to spare. Fold a crease into each and set to one side.

Cream together the butter and sugar until pale and fluffy. Scrape the seeds from the vanilla pod and add to the mixture. Beat in the egg a little at a time, adding the flour in between each addition. Add enough milk to give a soft dropping consistency. Spoon into the pudding basin and level off the top.

Bring a large pan of water to the boil. Place the greaseproof paper and foil over the top of the basin. Secure in place with string – you'll probably need another pair of hands for this one. Make a handle with some extra string.

Carefully lower the pudding into the simmering water, making sure the water comes two-thirds of the way up the side of the bowl. Cover with a tight-fitting lid and simmer for 1½ hours. Carefully turn out on to a serving plate and serve with hot custard.

Tip
Don't be tempted to lift the lid to check the water level in the first 45 minutes of cooking: it's the equivalent of opening an oven door when you're baking a cake – disaster!

'Have plenty of extra warm syrup at the ready if you have a really sweet tooth!'

Champagne and raspberry jellies

Makes 6 / Ready in 15 minutes, plus chilling

135g pack raspberry-
flavour jelly cubes

4 tablespoons
Chambord liqueur

around 450ml
sparkling wine

150g fresh raspberries

A wonderful way to end a fantastic night of feasting with friends. If you've not come across Chambord liqueur before, prepare to fall in love! It's a fantastic black raspberry liqueur that was just made to be partnered with Champagne.

Place the jelly cubes in a large microwavable jug and add 100ml water. Heat until completely dissolved and then add the Chambord. Top up with enough sparkling wine to make an overall liquid measure of 600ml in the jug. Allow to cool a little.

Divide the raspberries among 6 Champagne flutes and then pour the jelly mixture into each until roughly even. Place in the fridge for 2 hours or until completely set.

Tip
If you haven't a microwave, simply heat the jelly cubes with the water in a small saucepan before pouring into a measuring jug to finish off.

'I say Champagne but I probably mean Cava or one of those lovely bottles of sparkling wine from New Zealand. I always think it's a bit mad to spend so much money on Champagne when there are some great (much cheaper!) sparklers around.'

Chocolate-muffin and raspberry trifle

Serves 8 / Ready in 15 minutes

4 double chocolate chip muffins (about 250g in total)

3 tablespoons Chambord liqueur or crème de cassis

250g pot mascarpone cheese

2 tablespoons icing sugar

284ml pot double cream, lightly whipped

400g raspberries

500g pot fresh ready-made custard

chocolate curls, to decorate

This really is a quick assembly job of a dessert that is worth its weight in gold. Make it an hour or so ahead and then wheel it out with your head held high!

Cut the muffins into thick chunks and place in the bottom of a large trifle dish. Drizzle over the liqueur or cassis and set to one side. Beat together the mascarpone cheese and icing sugar and then stir in the double cream. Set to one side.

Scatter the raspberries over the muffins, reserving a good handful for decoration. Pour over the custard and then spoon over the mascarpone mixture. Top with the chocolate curls and the remaining raspberries and chill until needed.

Tip

The trick to making really impressive chocolate curls is to have the chocolate at just the right temperature. If it's too cold, they'll fracture and break, too warm and they just won't work. If you really don't fancy the effort, simply 'peel' a big slab of chocolate with a vegetable peeler over the top of the trifle.

'I've never been a fan of jelly in trifles – which is a bit of luck really as it cuts your time in the kitchen by half!'

Plum crumble

Serves 4 / Ready in 45 minutes

750g plums,
halved and stoned

40g demerara sugar

for the topping

100g plain flour

75g butter, cubed

75g demerara sugar

25g flaked almonds

to serve

fresh ready-made
custard

This simple crumble mix is an absolute favourite of mine as it's just so buttery and rich. Make sure you leave in lots of lumps and bumps for a great texture.

Preheat the oven to gas5/180°C/160°C fan. Place the plums in a 1½ litre baking dish, scatter over the sugar and set to one side.

Tip the flour into a bowl and add the butter. Rub together until the mixture resembles breadcrumbs. Add the sugar and almonds and squish the mixture into rough lumps – this'll add texture to the topping. Scatter over the fruit and bake for 35 minutes or until golden and bubbling. Serve with hot custard.

Tip

If the plums aren't quite ripe, add a tablespoon or so of fresh orange juice to them, then add the sugar and bake in the oven for 10 to 15 minutes just to soften them up a little.

'Once you've got this gorgeous crumble recipe under your belt, try it scattered over ripe pears and raspberries or with roasted rhubarb flavoured with chopped stem ginger.'

Index

chestnuts: shallot and chestnut stew
146, 147

chicken
chicken in cider, garlic and tarragon
sauce 118, 119
chicken pot pies 140, 141
hot chicken doorstep with Dijon
mayo 92, 93
slow-cooked chorizo and garlic roast
chicken 136, 137
sticky mango chicken salad 30, 31
chickpeas: Moroccan leg of lamb
with chickpeas 132, 133
Chinese belly pork with wilted
spring greens 102–3, 104
chocolate
chocolate beetroot cake 166, 167
chocolate bourbon pots 160, 161
chocolate-muffin and raspberry
trifle 174, 175
chorizo sausages
garlicky prawn, clam and chorizo
pot 110, 111
slow-cooked chorizo and garlic
roast chicken 136, 137
soft-boiled eggs with chorizo crisps,
asparagus and warm bread 48, 49
cider: chicken in cider, garlic and
tarragon sauce 118, 119
clams: garlicky prawn, clam and
chorizo pot 110, 111
clementines: honeyed citrus fruits 46, 47
coconut: mussels in coconut broth 82, 83
coriander: seafood linguine with
coriander pesto 100, 101
cream cheese: smoked salmon and
cream cheese omelette 58, 59
crumble: plum crumble 176, 177

D
dill: hot-smoked salmon fishcakes with
dill and lemon sauce 22, 23
Dolcelatte and leek risotto 24, 25

E
eggs
béarnaise sauce 124, 125
eggy bread with crisp bacon and
blistered tomatoes 52, 53
smoked salmon and cream cheese
omelette 58, 59
soft-boiled eggs with chorizo crisps,
asparagus and warm bread 48, 49
tray-roasted breakfast with
poached eggs 64, 65
Eton mess 168, 169
ever-ready lamb curry 34, 35

F
fennel
fennel and pear roast pork 134, 135
seared mackerel with fennel salad 78, 79
fish
hot-smoked salmon fishcakes with dill
and lemon sauce 22, 23
whiting with shrimp butter 26, 27
seared mackerel with fennel salad 78, 79
smoked salmon and cream cheese
omelette 58, 59
tuna niçoise platter 122, 123
vine tomato seared salmon with a lemon
and herb dressing 112, 113
see also seafood
flatbreads: aubergine steaks with pesto and
griddled flatbreads 114–15, 116–17

Acknowledgements

My biggest thank you goes to Tim Winter, whose photography never ceases to take my breath away and who gives me the confidence to think big! I just wish he would stop talking about chips.

To my agent, Clare Hulton, for her enthusiasm and drive and for seeing the potential in my book.

Thanks to Lindsey Evans and Sarah Hulbert at Penguin for all their support, vision and kindness. Thank you to the designer, Nathan Burton, and Janis Barbi for producing such a beautiful book.

Thanks to Paula and Rich for being so generous in letting me cook up a storm in their beautiful Dorset holiday cottage (which, by the way, is available to rent!): www.ChurchHillCottage.com.

Thanks to Jo Harris, who let me raid her lovely prop house without even batting an eyelid and who later stepped into the brink to help style the last few shots. You're a dream.

Thank you to the lovely Diana from Gardener and Cook and Laura from The Olive Tree, who let me beg, steal and borrow all manner of crocks, props and plates from their wonderful shops: www.gardenerandcookstores.co.uk and www.theolivetreeshop.co.uk.

Thanks to my mum for teaching me how to cook and how to love food. And I'd best mention my dad and my wonderful big sis, Sarah. You're the biz.

And finally, thank you to my fantastic friends for all the great weekends away that were the reason this book came about. Thanks for supporting me and for being just as excited as I am about this book!

Emma and Jez, Al and Steve, Shelby and Kofi, Sue 'my middle name is Anne' (thanks for your tireless support) and Graham (there'll be room in the pool for you!), Debbie and Anita at Candis for all their support, Heather and Jo for spurring me on. And thank you to my best friend Harvey. I couldn't have done it without you.